A delightful discussion held.

Tom Steffen, Professor of I
Cook School of Intercultui.

"Who do the people say I am?" is a question still part of any discourse and interfaith dialogue between the people of the Book and the followers of Islam. It is a novel approach to let the Messiah of the Book speak for himself with al Masih of the Qur'an for the purpose of bridging the gap and understanding the views held for centuries by the two peoples.

Ashkenaz Asif Khan, Principal
Zarephath Bible Institute, Pakistan

Wow! Jeff has provided a valuable resource for understanding the difference between the Jesus of the Qur'an and the Jesus of the Bible. Using a captivating narration of the two Jesuses on a journey toward Jerusalem and the conversation which ensued between these two individuals, the clear differences between Islam's and Christianity's understanding of Jesus are exposed in a manner that is respectful to Islam, honoring to Christ, and scholarly in its substance. Using story to convey important truths from both Islam and Christianity requires an expertise of the subject matter, and Dr. Morton is able to accomplish this well. It is truly a good read. The appendices at the conclusion of the book provide additional ways of exploring the differences, providing even more insight.

David Talley, Ph.D., Professor of Old Testament
Chairman, Biblical/Theological Studies Department
Biola University

When it comes to engaging Muslims with the claims and character of Jesus Christ, this book is the most exciting, creative, and evangelistically insightful book that I have seen in my life! These delightful stories will not only introduce the Jesus of the New Testament Gospels to Muslims in a meaningful way, but it will also equip Christians to know this Jesus in fresh and deeper ways. If you have any concern in reaching Muslims with the Gospel, this is a must read!

Abdul Saleeb, Co-author of *Answering Islam*

Jeff Morton's excellent work is a timely guide to Christians who are called by our Lord to witness to Muslims. His choice of a dialogue between 'Isa and Jesus as a method to instruct Christians about Islam is pedagogically ideal, especially for those uninitiated Western Christians who have little or no knowledge of this subject. I recommend it highly.

Rev. Bassam Michael Madany
Middle East Resources

Two Messiahs by Jeff Morton certainly is a story you will have a difficult time putting down. I began it thinking I would take my time, but I finished it in one sitting . . . a first for me! Cleverly written with wit and candor, Two Messiahs brings together the "Jesus of the Bible" with the "'Isa of the Qur'an" on a journey to Jerusalem. As they walk together the two "messiahs" talk about themselves, each referring to the texts from both traditions to back up what they are saying, and you as a reader begin to see just how vacant and vacuous the 'Isa of the Qur'an really is. I had to smile and even at times laugh out loud as the Jesus of the Bible brings out small but deftly handled quips concerning the inadequacies in the 93 references to 'Isa in the Qur'an. Nonetheless, I found myself liking both of the "messiahs," watching as they traded Middle Eastern proverbs, sparring at the other's beliefs, but I came away understanding just how different the two views of Jesus really are. When you finish the story, don't put the book away but continue on with the appendixes, which are packed full of hard facts and references to that which the "two messiahs" were saying.

Jay Smith, Missionary and apologist

TWO MESSIAHS

Two Messiahs

The Jesus of Christianity and the Jesus of Islam

JEFF MORTON

Transforming lives through God's Word

Transforming lives through God's Word

Biblica provides God's Word to people through translation, publishing and Bible engagement in Africa, Asia Pacific, Europe, Latin America, Middle East, and North America. Through its worldwide reach, Biblica engages people with God's Word so that their lives are transformed through a relationship with Jesus Christ.

Biblica Publishing
We welcome your questions and comments.

1820 Jet Stream Drive, Colorado Springs, CO 80921 USA
www.Biblica.com

Two Messiahs
ISBN-13: 978-1-60657-095-1

Copyright © 2011 by Jeff Morton

13 12 11 / 6 5 4 3 2 1

Published in 2011 by Biblica, Inc.™

A catalog record for this book is available through the Library of Congress.

Printed in the United States of America

Contents

Introduction 1

Prologue 7

Chapter 1 11
Introductions

Chapter 2 25
For Unto Us a Child Is Born

Chapter 3 39
One More to Come

Chapter 4 55
Wine, Women, and Song

Chapter 5 69
Jots and Tittles

Chapter 6 81
Boys with Beetles

Chapter 7 93
Did He or Didn't He Die?

Chapter 8 109
A Grievous Penalty

Chapter 9 129
The Last Hour

Appendix A 137
Physical Descriptions of Jesus in Islamic Sources

Appendix B   139
    Why Provide Descriptions of Jesus?

Appendix C   145
    A Summary of the Qur'anic Jesus

Endnotes   149

Introduction

Why Jesus?

"The Bible is corrupted, but if I believed anything in it, it would be the words of Jesus."

I first heard this many years ago from an American convert to Islam. I have since heard this statement or variants of it many times. It is a remarkable statement for Muslims to make because the popular Islamic position, heard from college student to engineer, plumber to lawyer, is that while the Bible has some truth in it, essentially it is human foolishness. So, since Muslims begin with the premise of an altered and corrupted Bible, a premise ingrained in them by their teachers and scholars and ironically *not* by the Qur'an itself, a Muslim who agrees to listen to the words of Jesus as found in the Bible presents the Christian with a real opportunity that must not be missed.

These opportunities set me thinking how it might be best to proclaim the gospel using only the words of Jesus. I was immediately drawn to

Luke's account of Jesus' meeting with two of his bewildered disciples on the way to Emmaus (Luke 24:13–35). I wish I'd been there to hear Jesus explaining the purpose of his coming, life, death, and resurrection and, "beginning with Moses and with all the prophets," showing how Messiah is related to all of Scripture. Now that's a chapter I wish Luke would have included. It might have precluded the writing of this book!

In my own relationship with Muslims, I often use the words of Jesus from the Gospels rather than citing the much-maligned and misunderstood Paul. There is rich material for Muslims in the miracles and healings of Jesus, his parables, the Sermon on the Mount, and simple accounts of first-century Jews and Gentiles. Christians, wake up! We must put the words of Jesus to work among Muslims.

Some readers may be thinking, "But Paul's words are just as much Scripture as those of Jesus." I fully agree. The entire Bible is inspired by God. My goal, however, is to discover which words we can use to our advantage when speaking to Muslims, and I believe it is the words of Jesus which will make clear to them who he is.

My purpose in creating a fictional account of Jesus and his doppelganger is not for the immediate benefit of Muslims. That is, this is not a manual for the proclamation of the gospel. Rather, it is my desire first to help Christians, not so much to understand biblical christology (this has been accomplished in many other books) but to begin to understand Islamic christology. I want to address the differences between the Jesus of the Bible and the Jesus of Islamic sources: the Qur'an, the traditions,[1] biography,[2] and many of the sayings attributed to Jesus by Muslim scholars.

I often hear Muslims say, "I love Jesus. I can't be a true Muslim if I do not love him." That can be a distressing statement for Christians, because we think we have cornered the market on Jesus. (In case you did not know, there is a version of Jesus in almost all the world's religions, including the more familiar Jesus of Mormonism and Jesus of the Watchtower.) As a missionary, professor, and lifelong student of Islam, I am troubled by the anxiety this brings to Christians. The problem is not so much that

Christians do not understand who Jesus is, but that Christians do not understand what a Muslim means by "I love Jesus."

My second purpose is to present a non-systematic comparison of two worldviews in constant collision. By *non-systematic* I really mean that I am not simply setting up categories for comparison, but I am letting the nature of a story full of conversation direct the topics for consideration. It is my hope to work through various issues of importance without being too pedantic in my prose. I believe stories often facilitate this better than a strict verse-by-verse or characteristic-by-characteristic comparison.

Why Now?

Muslims are making themselves publicly accessible in the United States. They have an agenda and it is important that we understand it. First, they wish to be seen as authentic Muslims and not as radical jihadists who explode buildings, planes, trains, and innocent bystanders. There is a concerted effort by Muslim political and social organizations such as the Council on American Islamic Relations (CAIR), the Islamic Society of North America (ISNA), the Islamic Council of North America (ICNA), and the Muslim Student Association (MSA), to offer to the American public the image of a peaceful, holistic religion within the fold of the American Judeo-Christian worldview. You will hear and read representatives of these organizations complaining that the jihadists have "hijacked" Islam or misinterpreted the Qur'an. The jihadists are condemned by the above-mentioned groups for their acts of terror, albeit more often than not with some twinge of ambiguity. "Islam is the religion of peace" is a mantra we have heard too many times in statements against violence. In fact, we've heard it so often we are inured to it.

Second, American Muslims are concerned—or at least they ought to be—with the image of Islam as a non-American faith. However, in an ironic twist, the imams and sheikhs who speak for Muslims in America are overwhelmingly foreign. They offer a foreign face and a lilting non-American accent to a religion contending for a piece of the American religious pie. Therefore, it is my goal to present Jesus and his Islamic "twin" in such a manner that readers can make up their own minds as to whether or not Islam fits into the Judeo-Christian worldview. Can Islam be authentically American? Is the Jesus of Islam a Jesus worth following instead of the Jesus most people think they know?

Third, what other religion is there that is a polemic against Christianity? What other religion not only denies some of the essential doctrines of Christianity, but even commands people not to believe these ideas? Hinduism is ambivalent about Jesus' being the incarnated God. After all, there are many avatars of Vishnu, virtual incarnations of the god. What's another incarnation? Buddhism is not concerned with whether or not there is a god; if Jesus is the incarnated God, that is not a problem. In fact, there are books on the market today that elucidate the possibility of being both Buddhist and Christian. Taoism, Confucianism, Jainism, Sikhism, and even Judaism are not concerned with Jesus as Savior. The latter, Judaism, has only a few who preach against Christian doctrine. The organization Jews for Judaism is a reaction against Christian evangelism and not an outgrowth of essential Judaism. Most Jews simply ignore Jesus.

That leaves Islam. Islam is the only religion that came into existence in a milieu of polytheism, Judaism, and Christianity, under the influence of a tribal society ruled by shame, honor, and revenge. Initially, Muhammad believed Christians and Jews would see the legitimacy of his prophethood. As time passed and this dream did not materialize, Muhammad began to receive revelations that put Islam at odds with the People of the Book—Christians and Jews. For Christians, the essential doctrines of the personality of God are denied in Islam: God is not a Trinity, he is never called Father, and he is unknowable. The uniqueness of Jesus is denied: he is not the Son, nor is he the incarnated, crucified and risen Savior of humanity. The identity of the Holy Spirit is also denied: the angel Gabriel is the Holy Spirit.

With all that said, it is important to remind the reader that Islam is not the enemy of Christianity. We have an enemy and he just happens to be the enemy of all Muslims as well. Our enemy blinds hearts and minds to the truth about God the Father, God the Son, and God the

Holy Spirit. Let's save animosity for our real enemy. Muslims deserve our prayers, our best efforts at evangelism, and our compassion.

Why a Story?

Why a fictional account rather than something a bit more straightforward, linear, propositional? I admit I am not a writer of fiction, but I confess to enjoying a good story. In my role as an adjunct professor I have been asked to teach on the book of Acts. It is with relish that I do this, because of the narrative nature of the book. This is how I attempt to teach it, too. Acts is a book full of wonderful stories, and it seems a waste to teach it as if it were a bunch of verses stuck together and bundled haphazardly into things called chapters.

With this in mind, I wanted to make the differences and similarities of the Jesus of the Qur'an and the Jesus of the Bible not simply understandable but also enjoyable. What better way to present comparative theology than to tell a story!

Further, stories create the very fabric of our inner life, family life, public life, religious life, and culture. The importance of story has been expressed well by Chinua Achebe, the renowned Nigerian author: [3]

> It is only the story that can continue beyond the war and the warrior. It is the story that outlives the sound of war-drums and the exploits of brave fighters. It is the story . . . that saves our progeny from blundering like blind beggars into the spikes of the cactus fence. The story is our escort; without it, we are blind. Does the blind man own his escort? No, neither do we the story; rather it is the story that owns us and directs us.

It is my hope that this story will serve as an escort along the treacherous, yet deeply satisfying and rewarding road of gospel proclamation to Muslims. For the more linear and propositionally oriented among us, I have provided a summary of the qur'anic Jesus in Appendix C.

With regard to transcription of Hebrew and Arabic, I have adopted a very simple approach. This is not a story that depends on a scholarly presentation of Hebrew or Arabic. I have only marked the vowels with diacritics.

Finally, how will the reader be able to distinguish between the two Jesuses? Initially, I considered using the anglicized Hebrew *Yehoshua* for the Christ of the Bible and the (again anglicized) Arabic `*Isa* for the qur'anic Jesus. *Yehoshua* seems a bit cumbersome and would be unfamiliar to many readers. I even tinkered with *Messiah* versus the Arabic *Masih*. In the end, and mostly for simplicity's sake, *Jesus* denotes the Christ of the Bible while `*Isa*, the Christ of the Qur'an.

Prologue

It is some time near AD 30. The scene is a dusty road between Emmaus and Jerusalem. With a steady gait, the journey from the one city to the other, between six and seven miles, is accomplished in two and a half to three hours. As we leave Emmaus, we are going downhill and we notice the region is hilly and lush with farms and orchards. Streams are not uncommon. Entering a valley on this path, which is not a paved Roman road at all, we notice small towns on our left and right. As we begin exiting the valley, we see ahead the Roman road, its solid stones offering firm footing for animals, wagons, and soldiers. We are now entering rocky terrain and for another half hour or so we are on a plateau, Jerusalem in sight, as we pass by scattered farms and the houses of those who are working them. Finally, as the city of Jerusalem rises before us, our journey is uphill for about half an hour until we reach the city gates.

Israel has seen dramatic events unfold in the last three days. Passover has just ended, a Passover unlike any other in the recorded history of the Jews.

But now I want to draw your attention to two men walking toward Jerusalem. They are moving slowly over the hardscrabble, rutted road. Engaged in deep conversation, both gesticulate for emphasis when not soberly listening to the other state his case. It does not appear likely at first glance, but this is a conversation that will shape future conversations and worldviews for countless millions.

The man talking right now is known as `Isa al-Masih ibn Maryam. `Isa the Messiah, the son of Mary, is draped in a simple tunic made from off-white broadcloth. He wears sandals to protect his feet from the potted and pitted road; tiny dust clouds poof with his steps. A man of ruddy complexion, his skin hue seems to change when entering the sunlight or shadows. It even seems to change depending on the complexion of those he is standing near. He could be described as red or brown. An Arab passerby might say he is whitish red. Not a particularly tall man, `Isa appears to be of average height, and has a broad chest, presumably from his days as a carpenter's son. His neatly combed hair is brown and reaches down to his earlobes. At first glance, his hair seems lanky, but up close it is clearly curly.[1]

The other man, drinking in all that is being said, is *Yehoshua* of Nazareth, a carpenter's son, an itinerant rabbi, and *ha-mashiach*. Jesus of Nazareth, the Messiah, has been on this road before, but this time he is headed from Emmaus to Jerusalem. Also dressed in a simple, nondescript tunic, this Jesus is not a striking man. You wouldn't glance at him twice if you passed him in the market. Oh, yes, he does have a few scars, scars you cannot attribute to his days as an apprentice carpenter. These are scars not found on `Isa's body. The hands and feet of Jesus are marked with ugly red raised welts that scream trauma. He also has a scar just below his heart. It's not one you would normally see, but it is there.

Through some quirk, crack, or wrinkle in time[2] the `Isa of seventh century Islam—the `Isa spoken of in the Qur'an—is walking side by side with Jesus, a Jew of the first century. `Isa is on his way to paradise rather than suffer the ignominy of death on a cross. Jesus, however, has recently risen from the dead and will encourage his followers with many appearances before his ascension.

In terms of the biblical account, this story takes place in the space between Luke 24:49 and 24:50. It is after Jesus' trip to Emmaus but before he takes his disciples to Bethany. For `Isa, it is after his near-crucifixion and before his return to Allah. For Jesus, the story might account for his sudden appearance in Jerusalem after the journey to Emmaus, while for `Isa, there is nothing in the qur'anic story that this story explains.

We will follow them on this gritty trail from Emmaus to Jerusalem. We will hear them dialogue, debate, laugh, and struggle to understand each other in this impossible intersection of two very different centuries— and messiahs.

Finally, I take full responsibilities for errors in theology and substance. I recognize my own presumptuousness in putting words in the mouth of our Savior. At the same time, this is a piece of fiction about an encounter that never could occur. After all, one of these men is real; the other is a fiction.

Introductions

Az-Zukhruf 43:63[1]; Bukhari 4:506[2]

When Jesus came with Clear Signs he said: "Now have I come to you with Wisdom and in order to make clear to you some of the (points) on which ye dispute: therefore fear Allah and obey me."

The Prophet said, "When any human being is born, Satan touches him at both sides of the body with his two fingers, except Jesus, the son of Mary, whom

Isaiah 9:6–7

For to us a child is born, to us a son is given, and the government will be on his shoulders. And he will be called Wonderful Counselor, Mighty God, Everlasting Father, Prince of Peace.

Of the increase of his government and peace there will be no end. He will reign on David's throne and over his kingdom, establishing and upholding it with justice and righteousness from that time on and forever.

Satan tried to touch but failed, for he touched the placenta-cover instead." ■

The zeal of the LORD Almighty will accomplish this.[3] ■

Two men, silhouetted by the setting sun, are saying farewell to each other. There is no embrace, no farewell kiss, just a nearly invisible look of acknowledgement by both, a most unusual goodbye for two Jews who have spent most of late afternoon and early evening together. As they separate to go on their own distinctive paths, there are some final words, but these are indecipherable as we are too far away.

How did it all come about? Two Jews, similar and yet essentially different, as you will discover, parting without a hearty hug of fellowship or the ubiquitous "shalom, my brother"? They do not appear to be enemies. In fact, they have been very polite with each other. Yet they are not the closest of friends either. Casual acquaintances? Traveling companions? Let me take you back to where they began their journey together on this road, the road from Emmaus to Jerusalem.

It's midafternoon. The intensity of the day's heat has come to its peak, but will, in these days of spring, quickly subside into a very comfortable evening. Here on the edge of the small town of Emmaus, the two men have just encountered each other and will almost immediately begin walking together.

They gradually become aware of the presence of the other. They are coming out of the small village from different directions. The silence is broken by the sound of a lark, then the yelp of a dog trying to find some food in the fields paralleling the road. Then there is the plodding sound of feet familiar with the long walk that awaits them. The two are walking shoulder to shoulder. They are walking from Emmaus, heading east toward Jerusalem.

The man to the right acknowledges the other, saying, "Peace to you, my friend."

"And peace to you."

The first man asks, "I assume you are headed toward Jerusalem?"

The other answers, "Indeed. And you?"

"Yes, for Jerusalem," he answers.

The man to the left states, "Well, it looks as if we may be walking together. I'm Jesus of Nazareth, tribe of Judah. What's your name, my brother?"

A bit startled, the broad-chested man answers, "`Isa . . . `Isa al-Masih ibn Maryam. My best greetings to you and your family, Jesus of Nazareth." With raised eyebrow, he asks, "What takes you to Jerusalem?"

"Oh, some business with lots of friends and family I need to see."

`Isa asks, "Oh, family business? And what type of business is that?"

Jesus replies, "My father was a carpenter, but I'm doing more than that honorable profession. I have many people to see before I need to leave there. And you, family business as well?"

"No, not family business, but other matters. You see I've just . . ." He hesitates. "I've just had . . ." He hesitates a bit longer. "Well, let's just say I've had a life-changing experience and so there are some things I need to take care of. But I'm not going all the way to Jerusalem."

The two travelers stride silently side by side, step for step, still sizing each other up. Neither is willing to be fully candid, at least not yet. Initial politeness and etiquette is more important than openness, anyway. In this culture, self-disclosure does not come simply upon meeting someone for the first time. People don't become friends because of a chance meeting or a journey together. Friendship is earned through countless hours of sitting, talking, eating together, and sharing common experiences. Besides, there are other matters that must be discussed first: lineage, connections (or non-connections, for that matter) to society at large, and social status. As two people explore each of these areas, trust can grow.

They are passing the final house on the edge of Emmaus. The road to Jerusalem is mostly uphill. It will not be a leisurely stroll. The landscape consists of rough hills covered with blotches of small bushes and shrubs. While there are a few oak trees to be seen, the hills are splashed with green grass and colorful flowers due to plentiful rain.

`Isa breaks the silence. "Nazareth, eh? I've heard that nothing good comes out of Nazareth." `Isa turns to Jesus and smiles.[4] It's the kind of smile that acknowledges at once the good-natured intent of the proverb.

Jesus returns the smile. "Yes, I've heard the same thing many times. It's a pretty good-sized town, perhaps upwards of seven thousand men, rich and poor, merchant and farmer. Our house was near the market. It made my father's business a bit easier. He made lots of yokes, stools, benches, shaved handles for tools. Things like that. I'm the oldest, so my father taught me his trade."

After a few seconds Jesus asks, "And you? Where are you from?"

`Isa answers, "Nazareth, too. Funny isn't it, but I really don't remember a lot about growing up in Nazareth."[5]

"It hasn't changed much. The folks are still the same: parochial in their outlook on life and firm in their commitment to Torah. But tell me about your name. I haven't heard a name like that before."

"I suppose it may seem unusual, but it's what my mother calls me." He looks playfully at Jesus and says, "If it came from my mother, that's good enough for me."

"Yes," Jesus smiles and nods, "that's good enough for me, too."[6] Jesus raises one eyebrow and continues, "Still, I'm fascinated by your name: `Isa ibn Maryam. Your given name is unique enough, but that you are known as the son of Mary is highly unusual. My mother's name is also Mary, but I am not usually called Mary's son.[7] I am either known as the carpenter's son or simply Jesus of Nazareth."

`Isa's eyes light up. "How intriguing! Yes, I am `Isa son of Mary. I know some think it rather insulting to be called by a mother's name, but it's certainly not a disgrace to be known as the son of a righteous and pure servant of our Lord."

Nodding his head, Jesus affirms, "I couldn't have said it better."[8]

`Isa asks, "There's one word in my name you haven't asked me about yet."

Jesus replies, "Oh? Which one?"

"Al-Masih. This is part of the name given to me by our Lord (glorious and exalted is He)."

"Sure, al-Masih," Jesus says, "like *ha-mashiach*, the anointed one of the Lord."

`Isa asks, "Yes, but do you know what it means? Do you know its significance?"

"I'm pretty sure I do, but tell me anyway."

As if reciting from a memorized text, `Isa says, "I am a messenger of Allah.[9] I worship Allah and the angels stand in my presence due to my high position.[10] That being so, let me state right away and with great emphasis, I am not the Lord![11] I seek protection in Allah from the accursed Satan!"

"Sorry," Jesus interrupts, obviously drinking in all that `Isa is saying. "I noticed that your name, al-Masih, is the Arabic transliteration of *ha-mashiach*. See what I mean about names moving from one language to another? But," Jesus pauses, "that's not my question." Another pause and then he asks, "Why are you called the Messiah?"

`Isa grins and says, "It's part of my name! It's like a title. It's an honorific. As some are called *sheikh* or *emir*, I'm called Messiah because Allah blessed me.[12] I am Messiah to the Jews, but I am submitted to our Lord in Islam."

Jesus rubs his left arm at the bicep and remarks, "I've never heard that word before."

"You mean *Islam*?"

"Yes. I'm assuming it is your religion?"

"It is the religion of every child born.[13] It is the most natural of all religions and is, in fact, the only religion that pleases and is acceptable to Allah (most glorious is He)."[14]

"Do you mean—" Jesus begins, but is interrupted.

"What I mean is that Islam is the truth that there is one God and that Muhammad is his prophet. Allah is the most gracious and merciful master of the Day of Judgment. We owe him our worship, seek his help, and need him to show us the correct path."[15]

"And you are the Messiah of this religion?" Jesus asks.

"You know, Jesus, *masih* is a marvelous word. It means 'to touch,'[16] which obviously refers to the healings I performed, which were of course permitted by our Lord. It also denotes 'travel,' and that is exactly what I have done in my ministry. I have traveled throughout Judea and other countries, and I've even been on the pilgrimage.[17] So you see, as both a title and a name, it's a good fit."

Jesus replies, "I understand. It does indeed fit if that's what the word means. The Scriptures, however, do not use the word in either of those ways. There are several messiahs in the Hebrew Scriptures, messiahs who are called on to do a specific task, a God-appointed and God-anointed work for the benefit of the people of God. But the final Messiah, the Son of Man . . . well, he has come." Jesus, looking intently at `Isa, says, "I am the final Messiah."

`Isa seems to ignore the point. "Either meaning—yours or mine— the name fits who I am."

"`Isa," Jesus asks, puzzlement filling his face, "I still want to know *how* you got the name?"

`Isa is bemused. "It's what Allah called me when the angels came to Mary to tell her she would have a son."[18]

Jesus is tugging at his beard. It's a habit he exhibits whenever engaged in a deep theological discussion. "Are you familiar with the phrase *Son of Man*?"

`Isa is thinking. He gently rubs his nose with the index finger of his right hand. "Hmm. Son of Man . . . you've used it twice now. Can't say that I am familiar with it. Why? Should I be?"[19]

Jesus nonchalantly waves his left hand. "Not necessarily. It's just that this is the term I use most when speaking about myself."

"So, Son of Man . . . hmm . . ." says `Isa, musing, "but why this term?"

Jesus laughs quietly. "As I said, I am a carpenter by training. I apprenticed with my father, but by vocation I am the Messiah. Actually, I never called myself the Messiah. I preferred the term *Son of Man*. There are still too many of my fellow Jews who are expecting to restore the kingdom of David by ridding us of the Roman oppression. So I like the title Son of Man.[20] It's less burdensome. It doesn't raise expectations that aren't going to be met."[21]

`Isa is now holding out his right hand palm up, and begins pushing down his fingers one by one as he lists his titles. "If I may, Jesus. I am known as a prophet,[22] the servant of our Lord,[23] a messenger,[24] a word of Allah,[25] a spirit from him,[26] a sign,[27] a mercy,[28] a witness,[29] an example,[30] one of the righteous,[31] and illustrious.[32] I could go on, but I can see you are impressed, and besides, I've run out of fingers. Indeed, I'm the Messiah, the apostle for the people of Israel."[33]

Jesus states, "I am genuinely impressed. You are a man held in high esteem, yet a servant. I'm thinking this is a concept I heartily agree with."

`Isa nods his head. "You know, being a servant or slave of Allah (glorious and exalted is He) while at the same time an exalted, esteemed prophet is not a contradictory concept. In fact, in order to be fully submitted to the worship of Allah, it's necessary that I have all these qualities. They are gifts from Allah. They do not have their origin within me. Furthermore, to be called the slave of Allah is a reminder of my humanity. It's a token of simply being a creation of our Lord." `Isa takes a breath and exhales. "Yet how odd. We are both from Nazareth, both of our mothers are named Mary, and we even share the title Messiah! This is more than happenstance."

Jesus says, "Yes, it seems we have quite a few things in common. It's curious."

The two walk on for some time in silence. Each one is looking ahead and then to the right and left as they pass through the semi-arid region. Each one is ruminating over what the other has said. Quite a bit of information has passed between them in the short time since they met.

The sky is a brilliant azure and the clouds are high and light. The sun is hot, but it's the kind of day that would be a shame to miss by being inside.

Jesus breaks the silence. "Maybe you could tell me a bit more about yourself. If you are the Messiah, what do you do? What is your mission? What are you called to accomplish?"

`Isa nods and begins, "My ministry was earmarked by humility and obedience, submission and suffering.[34] I'm also the servant of the Lord[35] with the result that I will be lifted up and given a place of great honor.[36] In fact, I'm on my way right now to receive that honor."

Jesus asks, "Oh, what honor is that?"

"You know, Jesus," `Isa replies, "I wasn't in Emmaus very long.[37] In fact, I was just in Jerusalem not too long ago. My life was threatened and I was nearly killed, but because of my faithful witness to the truths of Allah, I am about to be taken up to paradise and become part of the company of the righteous."[38]

Jesus says, "That's quite auspicious. You mentioned you're a prophet—well, so am I,[39] although it was a title given to me by others. I'm a prophet, but it's not my main vocation. My disciples may have thought of me initially as a prophet, but as time passed they began to realize the inadequacies of the word. Just as they called me *rabbi*,[40] *master*,[41] and *teacher*,[42] they soon appreciated the fact that I was much more than any one of these titles."[43]

`Isa asks, "Really? A prophet, but more? How can anyone who claims to be a servant of our Lord turn around and think he's more than one of his creatures? Who's filled your head with these ideas? Assuming you have followers or disciples, was it an overzealous disciple?[44] Hmm. A prophet, but somehow greater? What could be greater in this world than to be chosen by Allah as one of his prophets, to receive his revelation, to transmit his message, and to offer submission to him?"

The road begins to take a fairly sharp incline at this point. Their pace slows accordingly. Off to their left the hillside quickly drops off to a rocky canyon rimmed with trees. At the bottom snakes a green trail of trees and bushes. There must be water down there.

After a minute of silent walking, Jesus answers, "Well, *greater* was your word, not mine. If a prophet is someone who brings the word of the Lord to his people, I'm most definitely a prophet. But if that's all a prophet does, well," Jesus shrugs, "I'm certainly more than that. My entire life was focused on a mission, a mission given to me by my Father. But the title *prophet* doesn't fully characterize my life. It's too limiting. It's a word that doesn't include all the work my Father gave me to accomplish."

The hill is definitely steeper at this point. The tempo has slowed considerably. `Isa's brow is moistened with perspiration, yet Jesus does not seem affected as much by the warmth of the day. Jesus suggests they sit and catch their breath. There are no trees for shade, but there is an outcropping of rocks on the right side of the road offering a place to sit that is mostly level and at least not in the middle of the road. They sit down and `Isa takes up where the conversation left off.

"All right, something more than a prophet. I can accept that. Prophet, messenger, servant, word, spirit, example, and all the epitaphs given to me," he chuckles, "would easily add up to more than a prophet. When you put them all together, they certainly encompass more than the office of prophet."

Jesus stretches out his legs in front of him, crossing one over the other. He puts both hands on his thighs and says, "You included the idea of a servant or slave in how your followers understand you. How do they understand the concept?"

`Isa responds, "I'm indeed the Servant of the Lord."[45] And then `Isa asks almost abruptly, "What is it that we owe our Lord, Jesus?"

Without hesitating, Jesus says, "Worship."

"Yes, worship!" `Isa says, nodding his head. "It's our complete submission to Allah (glorious and exalted is He) in recognition that he is the one true Lord and that we're his creation. My disciples rightly discerned that calling me the Servant of Allah was in recognition that I, like them, owe the Lord submission and service. My service to Allah really focused on living as an example before my people. I showed them how to live in submission to our Lord.

"And, in case you are thinking that being a slave or servant of our Lord somehow indicates bondage or being forced into slavery to our Lord, this would be a complete misunderstanding of my relationship to the Creator. He is my Lord. As a human being I can give no greater allegiance to him than to submit myself willingly to his service."

Jesus looks directly into `Isa's eyes and says, "`Isa, I'd be the last one in the world to argue with you about our duty to the Almighty. I, too, am called `ebed YHWH.[46] As the servant of my Father, I was called on to suffer,[47] to take on the infirmities of my people, to bear their diseases,[48] even to the point of offering myself as a ransom for many.[49] My cousin even called me the Lamb of God."[50] Almost as an afterthought, Jesus wistfully adds, "He was a great prophet."[51]

`Isa asks, "You had a cousin who was a prophet? I did, too. His name was Yahya, which, by the way, was the first time our Lord gave that name to one of his slaves."[52] Pausing, `Isa then exclaims, "Yahya! It's been a long time since I've seen him. You know, Jesus, Yahya was a very great man. He was given wisdom by Allah himself. He was devout in his religion. He always did the right and honorable thing by his parents.[53] Even though Yahya and I were cousins, he never called me . . . what was the phrase?"

Jesus answers, "Lamb of God."

"That's it," `Isa says. "*Lamb of God*. No, that's not a phrase I've ever heard before. What is it supposed to mean?"

Jesus explains, "It's really about my being the servant of the Lord, a servant who suffers and bears the punishment for sinners."[54]

`Isa says, "Well, it seems we are both the servants of our Lord, but we think about our service in different ways, I as being an example, you as being one who suffers. It sounds strange to me that our Lord would call on one to suffer for many. Allah (glorious and exalted is He) would never allow for one person to bear the sins of another.[55] No, I'm confident your notion is not found in the Scriptures. Moses writes many things about sacrifices, forgiveness, and atonement, but the only time a human was offered was when our father Abraham was willing to offer his only son as a sacrifice. But even then, he didn't go through with it." `Isa shakes his head firmly. "No, you won't find one man dying for another in our Scriptures."

"Well," Jesus continues, "you would be correct if the bearer of burdens were simply another human being. Such a thing would be impossible."

`Isa replies, "As Messiah, I haven't been asked by our Lord to suffer or to give my life as a ransom. A ransom . . . who's been kidnapped anyway?" His mouth and eyes reveal another one of those infectious smiles. Jesus smiles back.

`Isa continues, "No, my work is living as an example, an example of one who is fully submitted to the Lord of the Universe. In fact, my greatest work really lies ahead of me. My work isn't done yet. As I mentioned earlier, I have to ascend to paradise in order to return and carry out the last part of my mission."

Jesus picks up a pebble from the dirt and examines it as if it were the physical embodiment of what `Isa has just said. "Let me see if I have this right. Your name is `Isa the Messiah. Your mother is called Maryam. You come from Nazareth and you have a cousin named Yayha. Let's see . . . and you also said your mission is to act as an example for your people and right now you're on your way to paradise."

`Isa is nodding and about to speak when Jesus remembers one more thing. "Oh . . . and you're not familiar with the terms *Lamb of God* or *Son of Man*. You seem very familiar to me, as if I should know you, but the things you've been telling me are . . . well, they're kind of fuzzy and vague. It's almost like I should know you, but I don't."

Jesus looks off into the nearby hills, imagining the scene, and continues, "It's as if I'm looking at my home, Nazareth—or what I think is Nazareth—from a great distance. There's the road through town. I can see smoke coming from the smith's forge, but it's coming from a different part of town than I remember. And there are the farms to the north of the village, but the olive orchard is a bit bigger than I remember. The town is in the right place and I'm pretty sure it's Nazareth, but those little details are nagging at me."

A gentle smile creases Jesus face as he reminisces. "My mother used to tell me, 'If you think something small doesn't make a difference, try sleeping with a mosquito in your room.'"

A grin begins to replace `Isa's somber gaze. "If truth and lies were places to sleep, the truth would feel hard, while the lie would feel soft."

The proverb swapping brings a twinkling to the eyes of each man. These windows into culture cause both to take a breath and sink deep into their individual pasts. Some time passes with silence taking up the space between them.

Jesus breaks the stillness by tossing the pebble away, saying, "Prophet, servant, Messiah, and messenger. I guess by *messenger* you mean that you have a message. How is your message related to any of your other titles? You spoke of being an example to the children of Israel. Is this your message?"

"Our Lord (glorious and exalted is He) has ordained that each community should have its own messenger.[56] The message of each messenger is the same, for our Lord is one! We bring the wonderful message that from the beginning—from Adam onward—the hope for humanity has been one. The truth for humanity's predicament is one: submission to Allah. The beauty of this message is that what Adam taught, Noah taught. What Noah taught, Abraham carried on. What Abraham carried on, Moses gave to his people. What Moses gave to his people, I have shared with my people. And what I have shared with my people is exactly what the promised one to come, Ahmad, will teach to the world."[57]

"Ahmad?" Jesus tilts his head a bit.

"Yes, the final prophet. You don't know about him? Hmm . . ."

`Isa shifts on his rock. It's good to sit down, but the rock isn't any softer for the sitting. Folding his arms on his chest he says, "My message is the message of every prophet: our Lord is one and we owe him our submission. Every messenger Allah has sent has been a human being who has followed in the footsteps of the previous messengers.[58]

"Among the messengers are men of distinction. Abraham, Isaac, Jacob, Noah, David, Solomon, Job, Joseph, Moses, and Aaron, Zakariya, Yahya, `Isa, Elijah, Ishmael, Elisha, Jonah, and Lot are all given distinction (may Allah be pleased with them all).[59] But in the end, our Lord will have to remove their books and replace them with his final revelation, the Holy Qur'an,[60] sent down to the final prophet and messenger of our Lord who is therefore accorded the highest honor."[61]

Jesus, listening intently, picks up another pebble and says, "You know, only one time did I call myself a prophet, and I was never called a messenger. However, my cousin is a messenger who brought the news about my arrival. John came in the spirit and power of the great prophet of old, Elijah.[62] He was the messenger of the good news that the Lord's path was ready. So I guess—and I mean this respectfully—your ministry is really closer to John's, in that you bring the good news of this final prophet . . . was it 'Ahmad'?"

`Isa nods.

Jesus continues, "You bring the news of Ahmad, while John brought good news of the Messiah's coming."

`Isa smiles. "Well, if you're not a messenger, does that mean you don't have a message? A messenger must have a message. You are not a messenger, so I am guessing you have no message." His nose crinkles a touch at the laconic suggestion.

Jesus returns the smile and, picking up another pebble, begins shaking it in his closed hand, along with the first pebble. The pebbles are clicking softly. "I suppose that logic is sound, but of course, *not* being a messenger doesn't preclude a person's having a message. The rooster announces the morning without being called a herald."

He stops shaking his hand. Dropping the two pebbles on the ground and dusting off his hands, Jesus grins and says, "I have a message of good news. My message is that the kingdom of heaven is in the midst of my disciples, that the renewal of the Torah and temple has taken place, and that forgiveness of sins should be preached to all peoples.[63] So, while I have a message, I'm—"

`Isa interrupts, "Wait, let me say it. More than a messenger?"

Jesus grins, "Yes, more than a messenger."

`Isa rises from his resting spot and says, "That was a steep hill, but I'm ready to go now."

Then looking up the road, he says, "I see more steep hills ahead. Come on, let's get moving before my muscles get stiff."

For Unto Us
a Child Is Born

Al-Baqara 2:16–22

Relate in the Book (the story of) Mary when she withdrew from her family to a place in the East. She placed a screen (to screen herself) from them: then We sent to her Our angel and he appeared before her as a man in all respects.

She said: "I seek refuge from thee to (Allah) Most Gracious: (come not near) if thou dost fear Allah."

He said: "Nay I am only a messenger from thy Lord (to

Luke 1:26–35

In the sixth month, God sent the angel Gabriel to Nazareth, a town in Galilee, to a virgin pledged to be married to a man named Joseph, a descendant of David. The virgin's name was Mary.

The angel went to her and said, "Greetings, you who are highly favored! The Lord is with you."

Mary was greatly troubled at his words and wondered what kind of greeting this might be.

announce) to thee the gift of a holy son.

She said: "How shall I have a son seeing that no man has touched me and I am not unchaste?"

He said: "So (it will be): thy Lord saith 'That is easy for Me: and (We wish) to appoint him as a Sign unto men and a Mercy from Us': it is a matter (so) decreed."

So she conceived him and she retired with him to a remote place.

But the angel said to her, "Do not be afraid, Mary, you have found favor with God. You will be with child and give birth to a son, and you are to give him the name Jesus. He will be great and will be called the Son of the Most High. The Lord God will give him the throne of his father David, and he will reign over the house of Jacob forever; his kingdom will never end."

"How will this be," Mary asked the angel, "since I am a virgin?"

The angel answered, "The Holy Spirit will come upon you, and the power of the Most High will overshadow you. So the holy one to be born will be called the Son of God."

Walking again, Jesus says, "So tell me about your family, especially your father and mother. Do you have brothers or sisters? Are you married? Tell me everything."

With a slight clearing of his throat, `Isa ibn Maryam begins the narration of his family history.

"It's a funny thing that when people read the Holy Qur'an, the book that the promised Ahmad will bring, not much is discovered about me, at least in terms of my family, my personality, and the like. But the Holy Book is very clear as to my purpose for coming."

"Ahmad. There's that name again. Are you going to tell me about him now?" Jesus asks.

"Let me answer your question about my family first. Then I'll be only too happy to speak of the promised one.

"My father is not one we talked about much, but my mother did relate one story to me about him. She was in the temple when her cousin, my father Joseph, served her and spoke with her from behind a screen.[1] At first he was disheartened to hear that she was pregnant, but that was because he didn't understand the situation. He thought people would think him immoral for causing the pregnancy of his betrothed.

"When my mother explained the circumstances of her pregnancy, my father asked, 'Maryam, is it possible for a tree to come up without there first being a seed?'

"'Yes,' she said.

"'But how?' he asked.

"'Allah (most glorious is He) created the first seed without a plant.'"

"Allah?" Jesus asks. "Allah, the God of heaven and earth?"

'Isa answers, "Yes, that's right. And so my father said, 'True enough, but the seed cannot grow without water, can it?'

"My mother replied, 'Don't you know that all things—living and inanimate—have their source in the Creator?'

"'Yes, of course they do, but to have a child without the help of the father?'

"'Yes, this is the case.'

"'But how?'

"'Dear Joseph, didn't Allah create the first male without a mother?'

"Yes, he did, but how did this happen to you?'

"My mother was very clear: 'Allah (most glorious is He) has brought me glad tidings of a word from him, whose name is the Messiah 'Isa son of Maryam.'

Jesus says, "Most interesting. Yes, my father also had trouble with my birth."

"My mother, Maryam (may the Lord be pleased with her), is a wonderful woman of righteousness. In fact, did you know she had a special birth herself? Shall I recount her story as well?"

Jesus' slight nod is all `Isa needs by way of encouragement. `Isa's countenance becomes more formal, more serious. It's as if his posture has stiffened just enough to be noticeable, but not so much that you would think it unusual, like the final seconds before a violinist who has been waiting for his opportunity finally to perform solo. `Isa has repeated this story countless times, and yet its familiarity is simultaneously sobering and satisfying.

He intones,

> "She who was born of the tribe of Levi, into the family of Imran, the father of prophet Moses and his brother Aaron (may Our Lord be pleased with them); my mother's father, Imran, did not expect to be blessed by the Creator (glorious and exalted is He) with the bright face of child. Anna, the mother of my mother, pleaded with the Compassionate and Merciful One, 'Give me a child and I will dedicate him to your service.' Anna was pleasantly surprised by arrival of my mother."[2]

Changing his rhythm and intonation to a conversational pitch, `Isa continues, "My grandmother named her daughter Maryam and asked the Almighty to protect her and any children she might have from the Satan. There was much to celebrate at the birth: a healthy baby, a righteous mother, an obedient father, a bright future, and a promise from our Lord (glorious and exalted is He). But my grandmother also remembered her promise that her child was to be dedicated to our Lord.

"Of course, as a woman, my mother could not be given to our Lord for service in the temple."

Jesus nods knowingly.

`Isa's hands begin gently punctuating his story now. "So she was commended into the responsible and loving hands of Zakariya, a priest of our Lord. Zakariya loved my mother and desired to take proper care of her. And, as Zakariya often told me, every time he went to my mother's room to take her food, he discovered Allah had miraculously supplied her with what she required."

"Ahh," says Jesus, "like the manna for the Israelites or the meat for Elijah."

`Isa carries on as if uninterrupted, "My mother grew to be a chosen and pure woman of Allah. She was, in fact, chosen from among all the women of every nation. She was honored to have the glad tidings of a word from Allah (most gracious is He) placed within her womb. The Lord said, 'Be!' and I came into existence.

Jesus asks, "'Glad tidings?' That sounds like a greeting. Did the Almighty send a greeting or did he say, 'Be'? Was he there in the room with her? But why would he send greetings if he were present?"

"No!" `Isa exclaims. "Well, yes," `Isa hesitates. "No, he wasn't in the room with my mother. He sent the Holy Spirit, the angel Gabriel. It was Gabriel by the permission of Allah (most exalted is He) who breathed upon her. This is how she become pregnant with me."

And then he adds, "Don't make things so complicated Jesus! The Lord named me Messiah `Isa son of Maryam. He promised my mother that I would be held in high honor both on earth and in heaven, fulfilling the promise to my grandmother. Furthermore, the Lord of the Universe foretold that I would speak as a child, and then as a man that I was to become one of the righteous."[3]

"You spoke as an infant?" Jesus asks.

"You find it difficult to believe? I don't see why. Did Moses (the blessings of Allah be upon him) part the Red Sea?[4] Did Solomon (the blessings of Allah be upon him) speak to the ants?[5] If these things can happen, isn't it easy enough for Allah (most glorious is He) to cause me to speak as a mere infant if it brings him glory?"

"True enough," Jesus says, "the Creator of the universe can certainly do these things. I'm not doubting the power of God, but I have never heard such a thing."

"If you must know, I was not the only child to speak at such a young age. There were also two others: one was the child of a shepherd and a woman of loose repute, and the other was a Jewish child."[6]

"These are incredible stories that have completely escaped my attention," Jesus says, "and I try to keep up with such things!"

"Well, my mother found the entire birth hard to believe, too. No, she didn't doubt what the Lord told her. She believed him, but she was confused as to how she would become pregnant. She was a virgin, after all! It was then that the Lord (glorious and exalted is He) created me inside my mother!"

"This is indeed an interesting story," Jesus interrupts, "but I have to know something. You say that the Creator's word came inside your mother. I guess that makes you the Word of God, right?"

`Isa stops and turns, facing Jesus. "Not if you mean that I'm some kind of deity! No, that's what some of my followers say. I am a word *from* God because he commanded me that I come into existence . . . and it happened! The same is true for Adam (may our Lord be pleased with him). Just as he was created from dust, so am I. Look at me, touch me, listen to me. I am flesh and blood, as are you. I get hungry and tired like anyone. Our Lord said, 'Be!' and I came to be."

`Isa is shaking his head with some force now, his hands equally channeling his emotions. "No, no, may it never be said that I am anything but a man, a prophet, one of our Lord's righteous creations![7] In fact, I happen to know that on the final day, Allah (most glorious is He) will call me to stand before him."

They begin their slow gait again. Their walk is at a leisurely pace, owing to the incline of the road. `Isa is perspiring. A palm tree is just up ahead, its broad fronds offering the traveler some welcome shade. `Isa suggests they sit under the palm. They sit silently for a minute or two in the bit of grass under the palm, appreciating the cooler temperature offered by the tree. No dates will appear for another three or four months, but the shade is as refreshing as a handful of freshly picked, tree-ripened fruit.

Jesus finally turns to `Isa. "I understand the importance of your title *a word from God*. You've expressed it clearly. I do have another question, though."

"That's fine," `Isa replies. "Just don't forget that I want to hear your story, too."

Jesus smiles. "What happened to you and your mother after your birth? You know, my mother was a virgin as well."

"You . . . your mother a virgin?" `Isa interrupts. "That's amazing. We share quite a few uncommon things in common!"

"Yes," Jesus continues, "and I'm sure you know it wouldn't be easy for a pregnant virgin—that term takes some getting used to—walking around town with the story that you are pregnant by the Holy Spirit. Most of the men would eye you lecherously, and the women would give you as close to the evil eye as they could muster. So what did happen after you were born?"

A slight breeze rustles the palm fronds of the tree above them. `Isa, legs folded underneath him, straightens out the tunic in his lap and begins his explanation. "You're right, of course. My mother was villainized by the local folks. 'A virgin birth?' they asked. 'It's unheard of! What a fanciful tale to hide your sin,' they'd say. But my mother would have the final say!"

`Isa places his left hand on the trunk of the palm tree, and, patting it, he says, "You know, I was born under a palm tree. When my mother was ready to deliver me, she found a palm tree to sit under. She told me years later it was a beautiful spot: lovely grass, broad palm tree full of dates for the picking, and a small stream right there as well."[8] `Isa is pointing off to his right. "And so I was born under the palm. That same day I was presented to our people and by the power and permission of Allah (glorious and exalted is He) I spoke to them."[9]

Jesus' eyes and mouth open slightly in amazement. `Isa is encouraged by his reaction and his story increases in speed. The words begin to spill out.

"Here's what I said as a newborn baby . . ." Raising his voice an octave, `Isa says, "'I am a slave of the Lord: he has given me revelation and made me a prophet. And he has made me blessed wherever I am. He has called me to offer prayer and charity for my entire life. Our Lord has also caused me to be kind to my mother. So, peace is on me the day I was born and the day I die and the day I shall be raised up to life again!'"

He stops his story with breathless anticipation of Jesus' response. Jesus is thinking hard about such marvelous events.

Jesus begins slowly, "You say you were born under a palm tree that had dates on it?"

`Isa almost grins. "Yes, lots of luscious, sweet, delectable dates. Our Lord told my mother to shake the tree and she would be able to eat those that fell on the grass."

With a twinkle in his eye, Jesus says, "You know, of course . . ." He hesitates, sighs slightly, and says, "Well, of course you know that dates only ripen after the last rains. That means in the middle to late summer, which can only mean you were born in the summer months, right?"

"Yes, of course, the summer months," `Isa replies confidently.

"Well, I think it best to remind you that if you are the Messiah, then you should have been born in the fall."

`Isa is staring at Jesus, but for just a second. "The fall? What do you mean? I was born in the summer. You need to explain what you mean."

"Here's the conclusion I want you to consider," Jesus says. "The Messiah was born in the fall, long after the dates would be ready for harvest. I don't doubt your story, but it's curious, don't you think? Here's a story that will rival yours!"

`Isa simply looks at Jesus. He says nothing.

Jesus continues, "All right, let me explain. First, you mentioned good old Zechariah. He was of the priestly order of Abijah.[10] He was a godly man. He would have served in the temple in the early summer according to the regular rotation of his ministry."

`Isa is listening closely. He says nothing.

Jesus is looking at his hands as he talks. He occasionally glances in `Isa's direction. "Second, just doing some simple math will narrow all this down even further. The Holy Spirit—the Spirit of Yahweh, not an angel—overshadowed my mother and I was conceived when my Aunt

Elizabeth was already six months pregnant.[11] This puts my birth roughly fifteen months after Gabriel told Zechariah he was going to have a son—while he was serving in the temple. Well, fifteen months after my cousin John's conception is early fall, not summer. In fact, if you think about it, since I was tabernacled in the flesh—ahh, I can see that interested you, but more about that later—and I was born in the fall, it only makes sense I would be born right around the Feast of Tabernacles."

It is `Isa's turn to be amazed. His eyes clearly express his amazement.

"Yes," Jesus continues, "one of my disciples likes the phrase 'tabernacled in the flesh' because I was born right around the Feast of Tabernacles. That feast is in the fall, as you're aware."

Jesus stops talking. He seems to hope for some reply. His explanation is offered as a matter of fact. His aim is not to bring shame, but to offer clarity.

`Isa looks up from his feet and, coming close to a smile, he says, "Jesus, I know you believe all of that, but you and I both know that the Holy Book of Allah says differently."

Jesus smiles broadly. "Sure. Your book says one thing and mine, something different. There really is no easy solution to the problem. I guess we all have to pick the hills we're willing to die on," Jesus said with a sardonic grin and a slight upturn in his tone. "I suppose we'll just have to agree to disagree on this point."

`Isa demands, "Don't give up so easily. Surely you have more reasons for believing I'm wrong about my own birth date. Come on! Give me your best argument."

Jesus shifts in the grass to face the other man more squarely. "`Isa, I'm not trying to convince you of anything. I think I'd rather hear that you understand my point, that you even appreciate it, and that it was clearly articulated. But, in the end, if you're not convinced, I can live with that.

"Besides," Jesus plucks a blade of grass and twirls it in his fingers, "I still have other questions about your story. You've said some pretty intriguing things."

"Yes, we can agree to disagree. All right, what's so intriguing about my story?"

Jesus' questions tumble out. "Well, for one thing, your name. You said you were given the name of Messiah `Isa." This draws a quizzical look from `Isa.

"What I mean," Jesus says, "is that I know you've explained your name, but I'm still stuck on your name being *Messiah*. And for another thing, you *spoke* when you were just one day old? And then you also mentioned your purpose in coming. And then—"

"Wait, wait, wait!" `Isa grins. "I appreciate the enthusiasm, but let me handle one question at a time."

"Sorry. I was getting ahead of myself."

"All right, about my name then. Yes, Messiah Jesus, the son of Maryam. I am the Messiah and Maryam is my mother. So there's no problem, right?"

Jesus says, "No problem with 'son of Maryam,' but I do have a question about the title *Messiah*. I guess it's not really a question as much as a statement. Messiah is a title after all. It's an office, not a name. It's any divinely designated person commissioned to carry out a special task. But you say it's your name?"

"Yes. In fact, Allah (glorious and exalted is He) even calls me Messiah, the son of Maryam. That is my name."[12]

"So you don't see the problem that perhaps the title Messiah has been confused for a name? This could easily happen over time, right?"

"What do you mean?" `Isa asks.

"Well, I mean this. *Messiah* is a Hebrew word that comes into Greek as *Christ*. If a person is not familiar with the Greek language and they are always hearing about how 'Jesus Christ did this' and 'Jesus Christ did that,' you can see how it would be easy to confuse the title for a name."

"No, I don't see any problem," `Isa answers. "People are often named for their purpose in life. My purpose is simply exhibited in my name. After all, our Lord (exalted and glorious is He) can do as he pleases. I'm sure you'd agree to that, right?"

Jesus answers, "Absolutely. My Father is not in the business
ing even small errors or of being confused in the slightest."

"So, your other question was about the fact that I was born _____ _
palm tree?"

Jesus nods, but remains silent. He is looking at his dust-covered feet.
He brings both legs under him so that they are crossed. Looking up, he
purses his lips, saying, "The entire scenario of being born under a palm
tree, speaking on your first day, that whole thing—these stories won't
be found in Christian writings until at least a hundred years after my
ascension and long before the appearance of the Qur'an.[13] Isn't it curious
that the qur'anic details of your birth are originally found in documents
created by overactive imaginations?"

'Isa gets up from the grass and squats on his haunches, his arms
hugging his knees. "Truth can be found in many books. The final truth,
of course, arrives in the revelation handed down to Muhammad. Is
Allah's Holy Book the only depository of truth? We both know that's not
true. The Torah, the Psalms, and the Gospel were revealed by our Lord.
The Magians have a book that has some truth.[14] Of course, each of these
books is in need of correction, but the fact of the matter is that truth is
where you find it, one hundred percent in the Qur'an, and here and there
in jots and tittles in other places."

Jesus perks up at the mention of the Torah and the Psalms. "Jots
and tittles! I'd love to discuss that. But for now it seems to me you're
forgetting one basic fact."

With the hint of an arched eyebrow, 'Isa replies, "And that is?"

"The fact is that your Holy Book claims to be a direct revelation from
the Creator based on a perfect book in heaven.[15] Yet the book contains
stories that are not found in other Scriptures revealed by the Creator, but
in books that aren't considered divine by either your followers or mine!"

'Isa replies, "That doesn't negate the fact that we both agree truth
is found where it is found. In this case, my birth story corroborates the
story as it is written in other sources. This is a marvel and a wonder: the
Lord is the best of arrangers and planners."

"I think," Jesus muses, "we are going to make lots of 'let's agree to disagree' pacts on our journey together!"

`Isa agrees with a nod. "Yes, I think you're right."

`Isa is examining his sandals, making a slight adjustment in the strap on one of them. He leans back against the palm tree. The two remain silent, drinking in the simple pleasures of a spring day.

Jesus begins again, "I know I'm asking questions haphazardly, but at the very beginning of your story you said the Holy Book doesn't say much about you personally, but does speak about your purpose. Help me understand what you mean in light of all we've been discussing. What is your purpose? Why were you sent?"

"Jesus, I thought you'd never ask," `Isa exclaims. "First and foremost, I am the final Jewish prophet to the Jews[16] before the coming of Muhammad, the ultimate prophet and messenger (peace and blessings be upon him).[17] I commanded my people to fear Allah (exalted and glorious is He) and obey me.[18] I performed miracles by the permission of our Lord, all with the aim of providing an example of a righteous life.[19] I modeled for my people how they ought to live their own lives.[20] Although very few believed in my message, I was not altogether unsuccessful.[21] For the last few years I have been teaching, preaching, warning, commanding, and living in the footsteps of the great prophets Adam, Noah, Abraham, and Moses (peace and blessing be upon all of them). And so, as all the prophets before me have done, I am calling people back to our Lord, and in so doing I have prepared the way for the coming of the final messenger and prophet!"[22]

Jesus joins `Isa in a crouched position, also hugging his knees to his chest. "It's as clear of an explanation as I could've hoped for."

"Good, but what about you? Surely your purpose is important for me to know, right?" `Isa asks. "We both seem to be the Anointed One of the Creator for Israel? Isn't your life an example for the disciples?"

Jesus is pensive. "Well, yes and no," he answers. "Of course, as a rabbi I encouraged my disciples to follow my example. 'Drink in all the rabbi says,' the ancients said, 'and be covered with his dust.' Yes, I am an example for those who trust in me. But it doesn't stop there. I'm more than an example, more than a prophet."

`Isa stops squatting and begins to stretch out in the grass, his hands behind him for support, his legs straight out in front of him. He is keenly interested and senses a lengthy narrative about to take place.

Jesus picks up where he left off, saying, "Our mother and father were placed by my Father in the garden, but sinned when they ate from the tree they were commanded to leave alone. They gave up their honored position as stewards of the garden. They became afraid for their lives. They were guilty of breaking my Father's commandment. But where there is punishment, shame and fear, my Father is merciful . . ."[23]

At this `Isa agrees. "Amina," he says, placing both hands over his face as if drinking in the blessings of his Lord.

Jesus nods and goes on. "My heavenly Father is merciful in that he promised our mother her offspring would do battle against the offspring of the serpent, the Father of Lies. The serpent's offspring is promised a mortal blow to his head, whereas the deliverer himself will sustain an injury that although painful—who enjoys snake bites anyway?—will not ultimately defeat the deliverer.[24] This promise has held firm. It is central to the long-awaited coming of the one who would finally defeat the Evil One.

"`Isa," Jesus pauses, "I am that promised deliverer."

Jesus is looking directly into `Isa's eyes. There is no wavering, no sense of mockery here, just the honest expression of one who is seriously committed to fully relating the accuracy of the story.

"In fact, `Isa, I have just now finished delivering, rescuing, and bringing out of exile the slaves and captives who were under the power of the Evil One, sin, and death. My purpose goes much further than merely providing an example of how to live. My purpose has been actually to provide the means to live—to live eternally in my kingdom."

`Isa replies, "A worthy purpose, I'll admit. But I do have something I need you to clarify for me. How is that you, a mere mortal, can accomplish what only our Lord is able to accomplish? In other words, if I understand you correctly, what you are claiming is an association with our Lord. Again, if I'm hearing you right, this association with Allah (glorious and exalted is He) is not only unacceptable, but untenable and an unforgivable sin of the worst sort!"[25]

`Isa waits a second and then asks, "So, have I understood you correctly?"

Jesus, still crouching and hugging his knees, says, "Yes, I think you have understood the implications of what I've said very well! My purpose is to accomplish only that which the Almighty could possibly do: to bring sight to the blind, to free the captive, to bring release to the prisoner, to heal the lame.[26] The prophet Isaiah foretold that this is exactly what I'd accomplish.[27] So, yes, you're right. The implication that I must be associated with my Father is most definitely true."

`Isa shakes his head. "This is exactly as the Holy Book warns us. I am only a man. I am like Adam. I am not in any way associated with Allah. This is a serious breach of his oneness and his unity. It saddens me to hear you say this.

"In fact," `Isa continues, "I know that one day the Lord will ask me, '`Isa, son of Mary, did you ever say to your disciples, 'Worship my mother and me because we are gods?' But I'll immediately reply, 'Glory to you only; I would never say that I had a right to be worshiped. If I had said it, you would have known it. You know what is in my heart even when I do not, for you know all hidden things.'"[28]

Jesus smiles. It is not a condescending smile, but more a smile of appreciation, appreciation for the honesty of a friend who is willing to state what he believes to be true, even if it threatens the friendship.

Jesus says, "A friend loves at all times and a brother is born for adversity."[29]

`Isa grins and, standing, offers his unscarred hand to Jesus. "We've rested enough. We should be on our way."

One More to Come

Al-Araf 7:157

Those who follow the Messenger, the unlettered Prophet, whom they find mentioned in their own (Scriptures) – in the Law and the Gospel – For he commands them what is just and forbids them what is evil; he allows them as lawful what is good (and pure) and prohibits them from what is bad (and impure); he releases them from their heavy burdens and from the yokes that are upon them. So it is those who believe

John 16:5–11

Now I am going to him who sent me, yet none of you asks me, "Where are you going?" Because I have said these things, you are filled with grief. But I tell you the truth: It is for your good that I am going away. Unless I go away, the Counselor will not come to you; but if I go, I will send him to you. When he comes, he will convict the world of guilt in regard to sin and righteousness and judgment: in regard to sin, because men in him, honor him, help him, and follow the Light which is sent down with him – it is they who will prosper. ■

do not believe in me; in regard to righteousness, because I am going to the Father, where you can see me no longer; and in regard to judgment, because the prince of this world now stands condemned. ■

"I think it's time I told you about Ahmad (peace be upon him)," `Isa says.

"Yes, the oft-mentioned Ahmad. I think I shall enjoy this very much."

"Many times I said to my disciples and the people of Israel: 'O Children of Israel! I am the apostle of Allah [sent] to you confirming the Law [which came] before me and giving glad Tidings of an Apostle to come after me whose name shall be Ahmad.'[1]

"*Ahmad* (peace be upon him) is Arabic for 'beautiful' or 'trustworthy,' for this is truly how people will describe the final prophet of Islam. He will come as a comforter and helper to all who will believe in his mission. He is the final prophet of the magnificent all Compassionate and Merciful One!"

"Hold on just a minute. You've really said a lot in just a few words. I need to understand more fully what you're saying. First, you told your disciples of the coming of Ahmad."

"Correct. I prophesied the coming of Ahmad as part of the covenant Allah would make with the Christians."[2]

"So, as I understand it, you are a prophet, right?"

`Isa nods.

"And then this Ahmad is a prophet, too."

`Isa is still nodding, so Jesus continues, "So how many prophets are there? And how do we know they are prophets of the Almighty?"

"Let me take these one at a time!" `Isa requests. He is slightly grinning and says, "Four things do not come back—the spoken word, the arrow, the past life, and the neglected opportunity."

"Well said. Please continue," Jesus implores.

"Allah has, in the past, sent a prophet to every nation."[3]

Jesus exclaims, "A prophet to every nation. Seems like a good idea, but doesn't that mean there are lots of messages and books?"

"No, not all of them came with books. Only a few came with Scriptures, but they all came with exactly the same message: Allah (most glorious is He) is one and we are to serve him.

"In fact, this was also my message to my followers, for I am submitted to Allah in Islam. I am a Muslim, one who is submitted in mind, body, will, and emotions to the service of the All-Compassionate One."

"Islam is your religion? You are a Muslim? This is the religion of Allah?" Jesus sends a staccato of questions.

`Isa does not appear bothered in the least, but says, "Yes, Islam is my religion. I am a Muslim, one who is submitted to Allah."

"But aren't you a Jew from Nazareth?" Jesus asks.

"Of course, but all of the prophets, while bringing the message of Allah to their people, are first and foremost Muslims. Adam, Noah, Abraham, Moses, and I—all Muslims. Each submitted to Allah (most glorious is He) in Islam."

"If it is true that you are a Muslim and a Jew at the same time, this must mean that your god is pleased with Judaism."

"Well, let me explain something first and then you can decide if that is true or not.

"First, I assume you are aware of the passage in the Taurat (Torah), 'The Lord your God will raise up for you a prophet like me. He will be one of your own people. You must listen to him. . . . I will raise up for them a prophet like you. He will be one of their own people. I will put my words in his mouth. He will tell them everything I command him to say.'"[4]

"Yes, I know it quite well. The Almighty was speaking to Moses about a coming prophet."

"That's right. And that prophet is Ahmad (peace and blessings be upon him)."

Jesus jumps right in with, "Wait. How did you come to this conclusion? How can Moses be writing about a prophet named Ahmad? None of the prophets ever named a prophet to come."[5]

"Jesus, slow down. I can explain the passage to you so you'll see that clearly Allah was speaking of Ahmad and not another prophet.

"Remember you asked me, What are the marks of a prophet, or How do we know a prophet from a false prophet? Moses tells us.

"First is the statement to Moses that the prophet would be like him, like Moses." `Isa is gesturing freely now. He seems to relish this chance to exegete the Scriptures.

"And how is this Ahmad like Moses?" Jesus asks.

"Actually, in many ways. Both Moses and Ahmad are law givers. Both are leaders over large nations. Both experience a migration of sorts and in that migration suffer persecution and misunderstanding from those around them."

Jesus asks, "Was Ahmad a Jew? Moses was."

Before `Isa can respond, Jesus adds, "Did Ahmad know his god face to face? Moses did.[6] Did Ahmad perform great miracles like the parting of waters and the ten plagues? Moses did. Did Ahmad know your god's name? Moses did. You see the point I'm making here?" Jesus asks. "It's one thing to compare Moses with your Ahmad, but what matters is *how* you compare them."

"Yes," `Isa says, "I see your point. But aren't you forgetting one thing?"

"What's that?"

"Aren't you forgetting that Allah (most glorious is He) tells Moses that the prophet to come will be from among his brethren?"

"Yes, the Lord said that."

"And isn't it true that the brothers of the Jews are the Arabs, as we both go back to Abraham? He was the father of Isaac, the father of the Jews, and likewise he was the father of Ishmael, the father of the Arabs. 'From among your brethren' means from among the Arabs."

Jesus smiles. "If what you are saying is true, this makes Ahmad the sole non-Jewish prophet to be sent by our Lord. No Scripture of ours ever records the coming of a Gentile prophet. I think you've overstretched the meaning of *brethren*, `Isa. The simple, clear, and obvious meaning is that my Father was going to send a prophet from among the brothers of Moses, his fellow Jews. Remember, he was of the tribe of Levi. Also present when God spoke were those of the tribes of Reuben, Dan, Gad, Naphtali, Benjamin, and all the rest. These are the brothers God refers to."

`Isa shakes his head. "No, I believe you're wrong. *Brothers* means just that: brothers, not tribesmen."

"That's fine. At least I understand now what you believe about Ahmad."

As the men traverse the fairly narrow road—it's more of a path really—the smell of lemon trees is making its way through the valley. Both notice it and breathe in the fragrance deeply.

`Isa leads out with another statement about Ahmad. "You know there are other places in the Scriptures that speak about Ahmad."

"That may be true, but before you get to another one, I want your opinion on whether a prophet who speaks for the Lord will at least know his name?"

"What? What do you mean? Of course the prophets know the name of our Lord: Allah!"

"Yes, you have certainly used that name many times in our conversation, but is it the name of the Lord who created Adam and sent Noah, Abraham, Moses and me, the Messiah?"

`Isa laughs under his breath. "Well, I don't know if our Lord sent *you*, but I know he sent *me* as Messiah!"

"I see your point, but that begs the question. Let me phrase it another way."

There is a large rock in the road that both men must veer around.

"Of all the prophets you are acquainted with, which of them used the covenantal name?"

"All of them, of course. They all spoke of Allah (most glorious is He). I really don't see what you're getting at, Jesus."

"You are making my point for me by insisting that each prophet knows the god named Allah. What would you say if the name Allah were not found in the Torah, Prophets, or Writings? And what would your answer be to why the name 'I Am Who I Am' isn't found on the lips of any of your prophets?"

`Isa is puzzled. "'I Am Who I Am' is the name of Allah? I've never heard such a name."

"No, I didn't say, 'I Am Who I Am' is the name of Allah. Rather it is the name of the God who makes a covenant with his people and reveals this name to Moses. There is a great difference. But . . . you know the story of Moses at the burning bush, right?"

"Oh yes, a marvelous miracle.[7] Moses was with his family when from a distance he saw a bright light. When he realized it was a fire, he commanded his family to remain behind while he went to see if it was safe. As he approached the bush he heard a voice: 'O Moses, verily I am thy Lord! Therefore (in my Presence) put off thy shoes; thou art in the sacred Valley Tuwa.' Our Lord went on to tell Moses how he should go to Egypt to deliver his people from the Pharaoh. 'Verily, I am Allah; there is no god but I.' So you see, Moses did know the name of our Lord. It was right there that he was given it."

"Your version is that Moses was told the name of *Allah*. The version I know tells us that the Almighty said his name was 'I Am Who I Am.' If anyone asked Moses who sent him, Moses was to say, '"I Am Who I Am" has sent me.' Then my Father confirmed that he was the same God who had directed previous prophets, when he told Moses, 'The God of your fathers—the God of Abraham, the God of Isaac and the God of Jacob. . . This is my name forever, the name by which I am to be remembered from generation to generation.'[8]

"So you see, `Isa, the name of the God of the Jews, the God of Abraham, Isaac, and Jacob, the God of Moses, and the God who led the people out of Egypt, the eternal name of the Lord of the Universe is 'I Am Who I Am.' Doesn't it seem strange that the prophets you mentioned didn't even know the name of the god they spoke for? Can you imagine a king sending an ambassador to broker a treaty in his name, but when he arrives at the enemy camp and is asked in whose name and authority he comes, the ambassador can only muster, 'I represent the king, but, sorry, I don't know his name'? Can you imagine the ambassador's receiving the respect he deserves?"

"But you can't be serious to think that the name of the Lord of Creation is a verb!" `Isa objects. "That just doesn't make any sense at all. His name is Allah (most glorious is He) and this is the name known by all the prophets."

"No, `Isa, it's not, for there are no prophets in the Torah, the Writings, or the Prophets who ever use the name *Allah*. In fact, isn't *Allah* really just a contraction for *al-ilah*, 'the god'?"

"Yes, but it's still his name."

"You can't be serious to think that the name of the Lord of Creation is a contraction!" Jesus winked.

A slow-growing grin spreads over `Isa's face. "He that counts his friend's mistakes will be abandoned by him."

Jesus replies, "He who is a slave of truth is a free man."

Both men look at each other and burst out laughing.

"So, are there more places in God's Scriptures that predict the coming of Ahmad?" Jesus asks.

"Plenty," `Isa enthuses. "You have a follower named John, right?"

"Yes," Jesus smiles, "that's young John."

"He predicts the coming of Ahmad when he speaks of the Counselor who is to come. He says he will come to convict the world of guilt, righteousness, and judgment."[9]

"And this is Ahmad?" Jesus quizzes.

"Who else *could* it be? Ahmad means 'praised'[10] and we know that your disciple originally meant to write *periklutos* rather than *paraklētos*."[11]

"I see," muses Jesus. "*Periklutos* is not even a Greek word."

"That's just it," `Isa responds quickly. "It is such a revolting word to Christians that they have completely deleted it from their Scriptures."

"So you're saying that the absence of this word is proof that it was removed?"

`Isa grins and says, "That's right. It has been completely removed so that my prophecy of the final prophet of Islam does not appear."

"You realize that this type of argument can, like a cornered snake, turn on you?"

"How is that?" asks `Isa.

"Simple." Jesus points to the farm on his right. "See the synagogue there?"

"Jesus, you know there's no synagogue there. That's just a field of barley."

"But what you don't know," Jesus interjects, "is that there once was a synagogue there. Of course, there is no foundation or any remnant of the building, but it *was* there. In fact, its absence is proof of its removal."

`Isa stares at Jesus. "That is nowhere near analogous to what is true about the removal of *periklutos* or the reference to Ahmad by John. You know you can't prove your point with an analogy!"

"Agreed, but it does illustrate that anything can be claimed by such an argument. You claim Ahmad's name was removed, and that the proof is the very absence of his name. I argue the synagogue was once on that spot, and that the proof is that it is not there now. How are these different arguments?"

"Oh, in a major way. You see, *periklutos* is closely related to the word *paraklētos*. There are just a few letters changed. That's quite different from removing the entire word, right?"

"How it was done seems immaterial. What matters is the result. If the snake is not now in front of you, that doesn't mean it wasn't ready to strike just a few moments ago."

"I think you are forgetting," `Isa says, "the reluctance of most people to accept that I am only a prophet and not the final prophet. Some of my followers refuse to handle this disappointment and so they will try many things to make me, as you say, 'more than a prophet.' But this is not who I am."

"Agreed. That is not who you are. But you continue to ignore the question about the alleged change from *periklutos* to *paraklētos*. There is simply no evidence for such a change."

"No, I completely disagree. The evidence is seen in the attitudes of those who follow me and who insist that I am more than a prophet. This is where the answer is found."

"Surely, there are more convincing passages of Scripture that show the presence of Ahmad."

"Absolutely. In fact, I am amazed you aren't aware of it, since it's clearly seen in the Hebrew of the Song of Songs: 'His mouth is sweetness itself; he is altogether *makhămadim* (lovely).'"

'Isa pauses for effect and repeats, "Makhămadim. This is Muhammad. 'This is my lover, this my friend, O daughters of Jerusalem.'"[12]

"Can we sit down over there?" Jesus asks as he points to fallen oak tree just a few steps off the road.

As they sit down Jesus tentatively asks, "Don't take this the wrong way, but you cited from *Shir-hashirim*. Do you believe that *makhămadim* (lovely) is the name *Muhammad*? If so, the passage you cited must rightly be translated as 'His mouth is sweetness itself, he is altogether Muhammad.'"

'Isa objects, "But that doesn't make sense. No, Muhammad's name is clearly present in Solomon's writings, but it is not translated as such. It is covered up by making it 'altogether lovely.'"

"What does *Shir-hashirim* mean?" Jesus asks.

"The Song of Songs, of course."

"Right, and doesn't it really mean the best song of all songs?"[13]

"Yes," 'Isa agrees.

Jesus leans back with both hands on the trunk of the fallen tree. "What part of 'Song of Songs' makes it mean 'the best'?"

'Isa directly faces Jesus, slightly annoyed, and says, "It's the *yodh-mem*.[14] We both know that. What are you trying to say, Jesus?"

Jesus looks at Isa and says, "Only that you know the reason *makhămadim* cannot be the name Muhammad. Only that you know it is an adjective that means lovely or desirable. Only that you know the *yodh-mem* is not a sign of respect. Only that you know that while it normally makes a word plural, here it intensifies the word. All I am saying is that you know it is not the name of any person ever mentioned by Solomon in his writings."

"No, I disagree strongly with you on this. It is very clear that Muhammad's name is present in Solomon's book."

"`Isa, let me ask you this. Because a word sounds like another, does this mean it is the same word? Doesn't the very al-Fatihah begin '*bismal-lah . . . alhamdu*'? Why don't you see the name of Muhammad there? It is the same root, after all?"

`Isa rises from the trunk, takes a few steps forward, turns to Jesus, and says, "It is the same root, but it is clear that it is not his name. His name is used four times in the Holy Qur'an and each time it is Muhammad."

Cupping his chin in his left hand, Jesus looks up at `Isa. "*Jinn*[15] sounds like John. *Rum*[16] sounds like the Muslim poet Rumi. *Rabb*[17] sounds like rabbi, but in each case the words are not translated as anything other than what they are. All of sudden, when it comes to the root *hmd* there is an effort to deceive? I don't get it."

`Isa is about to answer, but Jesus says, "`Isa, what is the Hebrew for urinate?"

"*Shātan*, of course."[18]

"So, why when this word shows up in the Scriptures isn't it translated as Satan? After all, it sounds like the Evil One, Satan, which is *shaytan* in Arabic. So it should be translated as 'Satan,' right?"

"You continue to come up with weak analogies to bolster your points. I don't want to argue with you over the analogy. You cannot convince me otherwise about this. I am firmly convinced Muhammad's name is found in this passage."

"So I guess those who systematically change Scripture in order to remove Ahmad's name missed this? 'Delightful' appears in many other places in the Scriptures.[19] Were these occasions also missed?"

"Yes, they were," `Isa says.

"All right, they were missed. The conspiracy failed!"

"No, there was no conspiracy, just the deliberate attempt to keep Muhammad's name out of the Scriptures."

Jesus stands up and they make their way back to the road. A small dust devil is working its way across the road just behind them.

"Look," Jesus says, shrugging, "for the sake of argument, let's say you're right. Muhammad is in the Bible. Muhammad is a prophet who comes in the line of Adam, Noah, Abraham, Moses, and you. Does Muhammad know God face to face as Moses did? Does Muhammad perform the miracles that Moses did? Does Muhammad know the name of the Creator, 'I Am Who I Am?'"

"No one can know Allah (most glorious is He) face to face. This is impossible. But, yes, Muhammad will perform miracles, the greatest being the Qur'an itself. Consider this: unlike me, the final prophet of Islam (peace be upon him) is illiterate. Imagine—an illiterate man being able to produce a miraculous book such as Holy Scripture! It boggles the mind. It is truly a miracle that a person who is uneducated shall deliver the perfect Word of Allah."

"Ahh," says Jesus, "just as a virgin would be able to give birth to a child, the perfect Word of God. Yes, I see the similarity there."

"Good, good," 'Isa continues. "But does the prophet know God's name as anything other than *Allah*? No. There aren't any prophets who know his name as anything but *Allah* (most glorious is He)."

"'Isa, you don't know Allah face to face?"

"No! I take refuge in Allah! I cannot know him face to face. First, he is highly exalted above anything or any description we can ascribe to him.[20] Second, Allah (most glorious is He) is with us wherever we might be.[21] If he can be everywhere and anywhere at the same time, how could he be known? No, this is too far beyond our small human minds. Third, and perhaps most relevant to what we're talking about is that when Moses asked our Lord to show himself, the answer was, 'By no means canst thou see me.'[22] Allah told the prophet to see his glory in the mountain. This was all Moses could bear to see. Even with this obscured appearance of Allah's *tajallā* (his glory) Moses (may Allah be pleased with him) was humbled to the ground before Allah (most glorious is He)."

"Yet," Jesus says, "the Scriptures tell us Moses knew the Almighty face to face. You even cited Moses' own words from Deuteronomy, and it is in Deuteronomy that Moses tells us he knew God face to face. Certainly, you don't think Moses is a liar?"

"Of course not. We simply need to understand what Moses (may Allah be pleased with him) meant when he said that. It is impossible to see God face to face and live—even Moses tells us that."

"True enough," Jesus agrees, "but remember it was Moses, unlike any prophet before or after him—that is until the Messiah came—whose face shone with the glory of God for having been in his presence."

`Isa is visibly tense and upset. "No, no! My face never shone with the glory of Allah! You are very mistaken about that."

"I'm not mistaken," Jesus says almost soothingly. "*I* am that Messiah whose face shone with the glory of God just as Moses' did. It is I who knows my Father face to face, as promised to Moses. I am that Messiah who did great miracles, just as Moses did."

Jesus lowers his voice almost to a whisper, as if he were afraid to disturb a sleeping child. "I am that Messiah who knows the name of the Almighty."

`Isa looks at Jesus as if he has not heard a word of what has been said. Instead, picking up where he left off, he says, "Now, with all that said, you mustn't think that Ahmad is not special. He is very special. In fact, he is the only prophet to have reached the highest heaven."[23]

"That is impressive!" exclaims Jesus. "He traveled to heaven?"

"Oh my, yes!" `Isa says excitedly. "One night, the Apostle of Allah was lying near the Ka'ba when suddenly a person—I don't know who it was—came and cut his body open from his throat down to his groin. The person took out his heart, placed it on a golden tray, the tray of belief, washed his heart with Zam-zam water and filled it with belief. Then his heart was placed back into his chest."

`Isa is looking at Jesus to see what his reaction might be to these words. Jesus keeps on walking, nodding occasionally and affirmingly as `Isa tells his story.

"The prophet Muhammad (peace be upon him) said, 'I was given an animal called Buraq, smaller than a mule but larger than a donkey. It was white and had a pair of wings. It was an incredible animal. Gabriel set out with me and before I knew it we were at the temple in Jerusalem. I went in, led some in prayers, and then we set off again until Gabriel and I reached the nearest heaven.'"

Jesus interrupts, "Muhammad saw the temple in Jerusalem? From Mecca to Jerusalem is no small trip. Did Muhammad describe the temple as he saw it?"

"No, not really," `Isa said, "but he did describe the nearest heaven."

Jesus looks disappointed.

`Isa continues. "He said he stood before a gate and heard a voice ask, 'Who is it?'

"Gabriel said, 'Gabriel.'

"And then the voice asked, 'And who is with you?'

"Gabriel said, 'Muhammad.'

"Then voice then asked, 'Has Muhammad been called?'

"Gabriel answered that he had.

"The voice responded, 'He is welcome!'

"The gate opened, and Gabriel and Muhammad (peace be upon him) entered into the nearest heaven. As they entered, Gabriel introduced the prophet to Adam.

"'This is your father Adam, Muhammad.'

"Muhammad greeted him, and Adam (may Allah be pleased with him) returned the greetings: 'You are welcome, pious son and prophet.'

"Then Gabriel and Muhammad ascended higher still until they reached the second heaven where there was another gate. Gabriel asked to have the gate opened. The voice asked the same questions as before and finally responded with, 'He is welcome. What an excellent visit his is!' The gate opened.

"Gabriel introduced the prophet (peace and blessing be upon him) to Yahya and me!"

At this, Jesus looks intently at `Isa, though the later continues with his story.

"Muhammad greeted both my cousin and me and we greeted him in return, saying, 'You are welcome, pious brother and prophet.'

"Then Gabriel took Muhammad to the third heaven. Another gate had to be opened. The same ritual ensued as before until the gate opened. Gabriel took Muhammad to Joseph. Muhammad greeted him, and Joseph said, 'You are welcome, pious brother and prophet.'

"From the third heaven Muhammad (peace be upon him) visited the fourth. Again the voice was at the gate. When the gate opened Gabriel took him to greet Idris.[24] Idris returned the greetings to his pious brother and prophet.

"Then they arrived at the fifth heaven. The voice demanded to know who was with Gabriel. Finally the gate swung open and Gabriel introduced the prophet of Islam (peace be upon him) to Aaron. They exchanged greetings with Aaron calling Muhammad a pious brother and prophet.

"At the sixth heaven, after the gate opened, Muhammad (peace be upon him) was introduced to and greeted Moses. 'You are welcome, pious brother and prophet,' Moses said.

"As Muhammad left Moses, Moses began to weep.

"'Why are you crying?' Muhammad asked.

"'I weep because another prophet, a young man, has been sent after me. He will have more followers than I.'

"Gabriel and Muhammad (peace be upon him) ascended to the seventh heaven. When the gate released, swinging open, Gabriel introduced Muhammad to Abraham.

"'This is your father,' Gabriel said. 'Greet him.'

"Muhammad did, and father Abraham said, 'You are welcome, O pious son and pious prophet.'"

`Isa senses that Jesus wants to ask him a question, but hurriedly presses on with his story, holding up his hand in a gesture of "be patient."

`Isa continues, "Muhammad's journey was not yet over. Gabriel led him up to a lote tree. The tree was heavy with large, ponderous fruit, perhaps as large as the ears of elephants. Gabriel pointed out that this tree was the farthest boundary marker of the seventh heaven. Additionally, there were four rivers, two visible and two invisible.

"Muhammad asked about the rivers and Gabriel said, 'As for the hidden rivers, they are the two rivers of paradise; the visible are the Nile and Euphrates.'

"Muhammad then said he was shown three containers, one with wine, one with honey, the other full of milk. Muhammad took the container with the milk.

"Next Gabriel told Muhammad (peace be upon him), 'You are following Islam.' With that, the angel showed him how to perform *salat.* Muhammad said he then heard the sound of creaking pens: a decree had been written that all Muslims were to pray fifty times each day.

"It was time to leave the seventh heaven. So Gabriel and Muhammad began their descent, but when then came to the sixth heaven, Moses asked Muhammad, 'What have you been ordered to do?'

"'I have been commanded to pray fifty times daily.'

"Moses remarked, 'Your followers can't bear fifty prayers a day. Trust me, I know. I tried as best I could with the people of Israel. Go back to the seventh heaven and ask for fewer prayers.'

"So Muhammad (peace be upon him) did as Moses suggested. He went back and the prayers were reduced by ten.

"When he came to Moses the second time, Moses asked him what happened. Muhammad told him the prayers were cut from fifty to forty. But Moses' advice remained the same: Go back and get the prayers reduced.

"Again, Muhammad received the reduction of the prayers by ten more. But upon reaching Moses again, Moses encouraged the prophet of Islam to go back yet again. This went on until Muhammad received the order to prayer five times daily. But still Moses was not convinced Muhammad's followers could handle such a heavy burden.

"'I have asked so much of my Lord,' Muhammad said, 'I am ashamed to go ask again. I have my answer. I submit to the will of Allah.'"

The two men maintain their steady pace. 'Isa is waiting patiently for Jesus to respond with wonder or a question, but they just keep walking.

After some time, the silence is broken by the rushing of a nearby creek. `Isa looks at Jesus and motions for them to go over and get a drink. Both men drink heartily and then sit on the rocks that protrude on the bank.

It is Jesus who finally breaks the silence. "I really would have liked to hear your prophet describe the temple."

"All he really said about it was, 'The prayer of a person in his house is a single prayer; his prayer in the mosque of his tribe has the reward of twenty-five prayers; his prayers in the mosque in which the Friday prayer is observed has the reward of five hundred; his prayer in the Mosque of Aqsa has reward of fifty thousand prayers; his prayer in my mosque has the reward of fifty thousand prayers; and the prayer in the Sacred Mosque at Makkah has a reward of one hundred thousand prayers.'"[25]

"You know, `Isa, I still would like to know what he saw."

"Why is it so important?" `Isa asks.

"Because the temple will be destroyed about forty years from now and will not be restored for at least several millennia."

"Hmm," `Isa says, "I see your dilemma, but the house the prophet (peace be upon him) may not have been the temple at all, but a mosque."

"If it wasn't the temple," Jesus asks, "how could it have been a mosque? Islam will not spread to Jerusalem until much later. Furthermore, let me ask, do you know when the mosque in Jerusalem was built?"

"How could I? I lived hundreds of years before it was."

"Yes, that's correct. Let me just suggest it will be built long after your prophet's lifetime."[26]

"So be it. It is not a problem for people who have faith in the prophet of Islam (peace be upon him), just like Abu Bakr."[27]

Wine, Women, and Song

Abu Hamid al-Ghazali[1]

It is told that Jesus went out one day to pray for rain. When those around him became restless, Jesus said, "Whoever among you has committed a sin must return."

So they all went back, except for one man who stayed behind with him in the desert. Jesus said to him, "Have you not committed any sins?"

"As God is my witness," he answered, "none that I know of. Except that one day, while I was

John 4:16–26

He told her, "Go, call your husband and come back."

"I have no husband," she replied.

Jesus said to her, "You are right when you say you have no husband. The fact is, you have had five husbands, and the man you now have is not your husband. What you have just said is quite true."

"Sir," the woman said, "I can see that you are a prophet. Our fathers worshiped on this praying, a woman passed near me and I looked at her with this eye. As she passed by, I put my finger into my eye and plucked it out, and flung it at the woman."

Then Jesus said to him, "Pray to God, that I may call 'Amen' to your prayer."

The man prayed to God, the sky became covered with clouds, and it poured. And so they were quenched. ■

mountain, but you Jews claim that the place where we must worship is in Jerusalem."

Jesus declared, "Believe me, woman, a time is coming when you will worship the Father neither on this mountain nor in Jerusalem. You Samaritans worship what you do not know; we worship what we do know, for salvation is from the Jews. Yet a time is coming and has now come when the true worshipers will worship the Father in spirit and truth, for they are the kind of worshipers the Father seeks. God is spirit, and his worshipers must worship in spirit and in truth."

The woman said, "I know that Messiah" (called Christ) "is coming. When he comes, he will explain everything to us."

Then Jesus declared, "I who speak to you am he." ■

In the distance, the two men spot several women, single file, leaving the creek. They each have a large clay pot on their heads. They are barefoot, splashed with water, and struggling with the large pots of water. The last in line is a small girl, maybe nine or ten years of age. She is having the hardest time of any of the party. Even though she stubs her toe on a stick, she maintains her balance and continues behind the women as they pad their way to their village.

Jesus nods in the direction of the women and says, "That's not easy work for such a small girl. I hope her father appreciates her efforts."

`Isa remains silent. After a few minutes, `Isa asks, "Jesus, what would you do if one of those women were to offer you a drink?"

"Take it, of course, and show my gratitude."

"And what would you do if the woman were a known prostitute? What would you do then?"

"Take it, of course, and show my gratitude," Jesus replies. "Curious questions. What would you do?"

"Once I was seen leaving the house of a prostitute. A person I did not know, but who knew me, asked, 'Spirit of God, what are you doing at the house of this woman?' I told him, 'It is the sick that a physician visits.'"[2]

`Isa stands up. Jesus follows, and as they make their way back to the road, says, "How true. I did not come for the righteous, but the sinners."[3]

"Agreed! But that being true, it still remains painfully obvious that the reason for our trouble originated with our first mother, Hawa,[4] who brought about the need for forgiveness by her error in the garden.[5] The greatest sin is love of the world. Women are the ropes of Satan. Wine is the key to every evil."[6]

"'Women are the ropes of Satan'? Hmm, I'm not sure I'm familiar with that saying."

"Oh, it's true, Jesus. Women are both a blessing and curse to humanity. You see, we know they are a blessing, for they allow children to be born. But they are also our bane in that they are able to raise in us the basest desires and lusts. Why, just the mere glance at them can take us down the wrong path."[7]

Jesus slows his walk and then stops, turning toward `Isa, who also stops. "Let me see if I've got this right. Our problems in this world seem to originate with Eve. All women are the ropes of Satan. One or two glances in their direction can lead us to destruction. Have I summarized you correctly?"

"Yes, you have, but let me explain a bit more. You know full well the differences between men and women. We men have an appetite—a sexual desire—that can drive us into a frenzy at times. A woman's sexual appetite is just as strong. In fact, it may be stronger and more compelling. Anyway, her very presence among men can make us do incredibly stupid things. So it seems reasonable for women to wear the veil, to cover their hair—the most sexually desirable aspect of a woman—in order to keep us men from servicing our lusts. It is the power of a woman over a man that makes her the rope of Satan. It is her innate sexuality that drags a man into the snare of Satan."

"I understand what you are saying. I agree that we men have a sexual nature that must be controlled. I even agree that women share some role in men's sexual expression, but I have to believe that, in the end, it is not the woman who is responsible for the man's behavior. A man can control his sexual desire because when I leave, I will not leave my disciples orphans, but will send the Comforter who will be the power of God in them."

`Isa takes up the walk again. Jesus is stride for stride.

`Isa says, "I remember one time long ago, I heard what sounded like mourning. In fact, it was some of the saddest crying I think I ever heard. Anyway, I was drawn to a man who was sitting at a grave site, sobbing and shaking with grief.

"Of course, my heart went out to him, so I asked, 'Why are you weeping, Ishaq?'"

Jesus looks up from the road and asks, "You knew the man?"

"No, but I knew his name."

Jesus nods.

`Isa continues, "I asked him why he was crying and he said, 'Spirit of Allah, I had a cousin who was my wife and whom I loved very much. She died and this is her grave. I cannot bear to be separated from her. Her departure has been the death of men.'

"Well, I couldn't just stand there and do nothing, could I?

"'Ishaq,' I asked, 'would you like me to resurrect her for you by the leave of Allah?'

"'Oh yes, please,' he said.

"I raised my eyes to the heavens and said, 'Rise, by Allah's leave, you who are in the grave!'

"Well, what happened next is really quite funny!" `Isa pauses and glances at Jesus to see if his curiosity is piqued.

"So, what did happen?" Jesus asks. "Did she come to life as you prayed?"

There is mirth in `Isa's eyes. He says, "The grave split open and out of the grave came a man who had been a slave. Now you may find this hard to believe, but there were flames and embers shooting from his nostrils, his eyes, and his ears. It was quite a sight, I must admit."

"That would be rather startling, I agree!" Jesus adds.

"But wait till you hear the rest," `Isa says. "The man said to me, 'There is no god but Allah, and Jesus is his Spirit, his word, his servant, and his prophet!'"

"So, the man was a believer and one of your followers, but sent to hell?" Jesus interjects.

`Isa ignores the interruption. "Ishaq, the man whose wife died, said to me, 'This is not my wife'—as if I didn't realize that—'this is her grave over here.'

"Well, this was something easy enough to remedy. So, I just told the man to go back to where he had come from. He fell down in a heap back into his grave."

"Wait!" Jesus interrupts again. "You sent him back? But why?"

"He did not belong here. His time was finished. Besides, I had promised Ishaq to raise his wife, not some slave."

Jesus shrugs his shoulders. He looks like he's wrestling with another comment, but lets it go.

"So, I went to the grave Ishaq was pointing out. I stood over the grave and said, 'Rise, by the leave of Allah' and up rose a woman covered with dirt. I asked Ishaq if this was his wife and he said it was.

"'Take her hand and get her out of the grave,' I told him. He did and they walked off together."

"Is that the whole story? Is there more?" Jesus asks.

"Oh, there's more. Yes, there's more! I heard from Ishaq later what happened. He told me they went off together where they could be alone, but Ishaq was exhausted by his endless vigil at her grave. As they sat under the shade of a tree, he fell asleep in her lap. He slept and dreamed of his great fortune in having his wife back again.

"While he slept, he told me, a prince on horseback with his retinue passed by. The prince could not help but notice the beauty of Ishaq's wife and he was immediately taken with her—and she with him. She left Ishaq in the grass under the tree in his deep sleep and rode away with the young prince.

"When Ishaq woke up he was quite confused as to where his newly found wife had disappeared to. He thought of all the evil that could have happened to her, and so he began to frantically search everywhere for her. He asked passersby, acquaintances, and everyone he came in contact with if they had seen his wife. He was finally able to catch up with the pair, and when he did, he demanded the prince return his wife.

"But his young wife said she had never seen him in her life. She looked at her new love and said, 'I'm your slave girl.'"

During the last few words, Jesus has been looking intently at `Isa.

"The prince then turned to Ishaq and challenged him, 'Is it your intention to corrupt my slave girl?'

"Ishaq was very confused at the turn of events and said to the prince, 'I swear by Allah that this young woman is my wife and cousin. I swear by Allah that Jesus, the Spirit of Allah, raised her from her grave and gave her back to me!'

"This must have gone on for some time, but as Allah would have it, I just happened to be passing by where Ishaq was making the plea for his wife. Ishaq saw me, ran over, and grabbed my arm"—at this `Isa grabs his left sleeve and tugs at it—"and pulled me over to the prince.

"'Spirit of Allah, isn't this my wife?' Ishaq asked. I said it was, but the man's wife said, 'No, he's lying. I'm not his wife. I am the prince's slave girl.' She was looking at the prince as she said this and the prince said, 'This is my slave girl.'

"I looked at the woman and said, 'Are you not the woman I raised from the dead by Allah's leave?'

"She proclaimed, 'As Allah is my witness, no, I am not!'

"What could I do? This was an affront, not to me, but to the power and majesty of Allah. 'Then give us back what we gave you,' I said sternly.

"She crumpled to the floor right there!"[8]

Jesus is nonplussed. He searches for something to say. "Are you in the habit of raising the dead only to kill them?"

"Jesus! This is hardly the case. Neither the slave nor the woman deserved their resurrection. It was accomplished by the mercy and compassion of Allah. And since neither deserved such mercy, they cannot be ungrateful for being sent back into the grave. I think you missed the whole point of the story, my friend."

"Yes, I believe you're right. Sooo . . . ?" Jesus raises his eyebrows and tilts his head slightly.

"All right, let me spell it out for you. Allah made the slave die the first time as an unbeliever. Allah raised him and then caused him to die a Muslim. Allah caused the woman to die the first time as a believer. He raised her and then caused her to die an unbeliever. And Ishaq vowed he would never marry again.

"This is the power of the woman, my friend. This is the power of a woman."

Jesus turns and begins walking. `Isa joins him.

Jesus finally says, "You have certainly opened my eyes with regard to your understanding of women. I cannot imagine being raised from the dead only to become a liar and end up back in the grave. This is truly perplexing."

Now it's `Isa's turn to look confused. "But what happened makes clear both that Allah is the only god who controls our world—I know you believe that—and further it makes clear the vicissitudes of marrying a woman.

"I myself never married. If one of my disciples asked me why, I often said, 'Be in the middle but walk to the side.'"[9]

Jesus again looks puzzled and is about to speak when `Isa says, "Yes, my disciples didn't understand my proverb either. I'm not surprised. They were so enthralled with the things of this world."

"Actually," Jesus says, "I was about to say that you really meant that you were in the world, but not of it, right?"

"Yes, that's right. I often said things like this to my followers,[10] things that were not always understood the first time I said them.

"I remember once after being tempted by Satan, I explained the situation to my disciples . . ."

"Wait," Jesus interrupts, "you were tempted by Satan? Before you go on with what you told your followers, let me hear the story behind that. It sounds fascinating!"

"Yes, I believe it is fascinating—truly exhibiting the power of Allah's mercy and compassion.

"I was set in Jerusalem by Satan. He pointedly said, ``Isa, you say you can raise the dead, so if you can really raise the dead it would be no problem for you to turn this mountain into bread.' Then he added, 'Such a simple thing.'"

Jesus asks, "So what did you say to him?"

"'Do all people live from bread?'"

"And then what?"

"Satan continued with his temptation. 'If you are the one you claim you are, why not jump from this spot? The angels will keep you safe.'"

Jesus nods, waiting for `Isa to go on.

"I said to him, 'God commanded that I not test myself because I don't know if he'll help me or not.'"[11]

"Really?" Jesus queries. "You know, when Satan tempted me I fought him off three times by reciting Scripture to him. There's great power in the word of the Lord."

`Isa silently concurs and adds, "That's my point exactly."

"But I notice you did not cite Scripture in refutation of Satan's two temptations."

`Isa looks intently at Jesus and says, "The Lord of the Universe has said: 'My servant continues drawing near to Me . . . until I love him, and when I love him, I am the Hearing through which he hears, the Sight through which he sees, the Hand through which he grasps, and the Foot through which he walks."[12]

"Ahhh . . . is this what you shared with your disciples that they didn't understand?" Jesus asks.

"Yes, but I can see you understand. It's too bad you were not with me during my ministry. As Messiah, I could have used someone like you to take charge of my disciples, to help them more, to be a sheikh for them."

"Hmm, an interesting thought, but it was not to be, my friend. My own path and my disciples were quite different from your own."

"What do you mean?"

Jesus slows down his pace a bit. `Isa matches his stride. There is a slight breeze from the south that billows both men's cloaks. It's a small relief from the relentless sun.

"As you know, Nazareth was my hometown. That's where I began my ministry, among the people of the north of Israel. One of my first sermons was 'The time is fulfilled, and the kingdom of God is at hand. Repent, and believe in the gospel.'[13] I trust you are familiar with the 'kingdom'?"

`Isa shakes his head and then nods, "Well, maybe not as you perceive it, but yes, I know about the kingdom. How could I not? I often taught my followers that anyone who has learned something, obeyed it, and then imparted it to another is called great in the kingdom of heaven."[14]

"Yes, on this we agree. The kingdom is not as much a place as our covenant relationship with the God of the universe, a permanent father-and-child bond that the Father yearns to have with every one of his children."

"We are in agreement," `Isa concurs. "I also taught my followers that I came to raise them from ignorance, to cure the disease of sin, and to heal them from the sickness of fraudulent beliefs and evil actions in order to purify their souls and raise them to the kingdom. It is only in the kingdom that we can be freed from the prison that is this world: a corrupted, vile home of the wicked, the devils, and Satan."[15]

"Really? This world is a prison? How do you understand that?"

"It seems simple to me: the person who wishes to inherit paradise will eat bread, drink water, and sleep on dunghills with dogs. A simple life, a life that is moving toward self-denial and away from the ostentatious, is the one that gains the kingdom."[16]

Raising his right hand in a sweeping motion to the sky as if to point out the vastness of the kingdom, Jesus says, "The kingdom! I don't so much disagree with what you've said as I want to emphasize that the kingdom is not about rules for eating or drinking, but about righteousness.[17] This righteousness is indicative of the bond my Father wants to have with each one of his children. The kingdom is this bond, this covenant, this understanding between Father and child. It is out of this tender and affectionate bond of Father and King with his child and heir that obedience is possible."

`Isa is mulling this over.

Jesus says, "I did not teach my disciples to be ascetics. I did help them understand the difference between denying themselves and asceticism."

"And what is the difference? I think I know, but what is your perspective?"

Jesus tugs briefly on his beard and says, "It has to do with motivation, intention, purpose, aim. An ascetic is hoping to gain an escape from the yearnings of the body—its appetites and lusts—and this is not a bad thing at all. But in escaping from the trappings of the body, the ascetic is assuming that the body is evil, that the body is the problem.

"I taught my disciples that the body is not the problem. Our problem is that we have brought shame on our Father by declaring our independence from him. We don't need what he has to offer. So, in relying on ourselves, it becomes easy to practice ascetic forms as a means of bringing ourselves closer to him.

"But again, this is backwards and does not address the problem. Knowing the Creator and honoring him is where wisdom is found."[18]

"Indeed, these are strong words! And like you, it's not so much that I disagree with you as that I emphasized to my followers that this world is not what we should desire. Just as kings have left wisdom to you, so you should leave the world to them."[19]

Jesus is looking at `Isa. Smiling, he says, "You know, I think I like you. You are not far from the kingdom."

`Isa returns the smile, adding, "I think you, too, are not far from the kingdom! You said earlier that you grew up, as did I, in Nazareth, and that you traveled throughout Galilee. With the important message you have, didn't you go anywhere else?"

"No. Just Galilee, Samaria, and Judah. I was sent for the lost sheep of Israel."

"Very interesting. I would've thought you'd make an effort to go to as many places as possible."

"That's really not necessary," Jesus says, "since I'll be soon commissioning my disciples to do just that."

"Of course, I see the logic there, but let me tell you about the joys of traveling to many different places with the message given to me by my Lord.

"My mother and I journeyed to the house of a man who was very sad. He told us his town was ruled by a despot who once each year forced one of his subjects to host him in his house, and this year it was his turn. He said that if the king was displeased at his efforts to pleasure him, he could very easily lose his head!

"So, I told the man not to worry, but to fill each water container he owned and I would turn the water into wine."

Jesus interjected, "Water to wine! Wish I'd thought of that."

"Well, the time for the entertainment came and I turned all the water into wine. I even filled other containers with food, some of the finest in the land, but as soon as I did this I told the man not to tell anyone it was I who did it.

"Of course, the king, when he tasted the quality of the wine and the exquisite delicacies I created, wanted to know who had prepared such a sumptuous banquet. The man put the king off as long as possible, but the king kept pressing him. Finally, the man admitted that one of his own guests had prepared everything.

"The king called me to stand before him. He asked me who I was. I said, 'I am a messenger from Allah and the food and wine before you all came from the blessings of Allah.'"

Jesus begins to speak, but `Isa, waving his hands, says, "Wait, that's not the end of the story! The king then told me he had a sick son. He said, 'If you heal my son, I'll believe in you.' Remember, the king was a despot and tyrant—and the son was even worse, if you can believe it. So, I said, 'I will do what I must do tomorrow.' That night my mother and I left without telling anyone."

"Wait!" Jesus stands still and faces `Isa. "Wait, you said you would heal the son but left secretly? I don't understand."

"What's to understand? The king and his son were evil. They didn't deserve kindnesses because they refused to show any to their own subjects."

`Isa takes up the path again. Jesus initially does not move, somewhat dazed, but within two or three steps he's back at `Isa's side.

"So, after my mother and I left the king's palace, we met up with a fellow Jew who was also traveling. As we became acquainted we discovered he had two pieces of bread for his trip. My mother and I were down to our last two pieces as well. That evening we stopped to rest and eat. I guess while we weren't looking our fellow traveler had eaten one of his pieces of bread. So we shared with him one of our pieces—it wasn't much, but enough.

"But when we put all our supplies together we had only two pieces of bread, not three.

"I asked him, 'What happened to the other piece?'

"He said, 'I don't know, but I didn't eat it.'

"I let it go, although I thought it strange. As we traveled through the desert of this country we came upon a shepherd. We were hungry and asked him if he would be willing to share one of his sheep with the three of us. He agreed, so we killed it, roasted it, and all ate together.

"'Don't break the bones,' I told everyone. They looked at me funny, but all the bones were intact when we finished that fine animal.

"I took the bones, prayed, and the others saw, right before them, that sheep come back together looking as if we had never killed it. It came to life when I touched it with my walking staff."

"That's some miracle," Jesus gasped.

"Allahu akhbar! After the sheep came back to life, I asked that old man if he had eaten that piece of bread, but he denied it.

"We finished traveling through the desert and came to another country where the three of us encountered a village performing a funeral. When we saw the corpse I asked who had died.

"One old woman said, 'The best man in our town.'

"'If you believe in me, a messenger of Allah (most glorious is He), I will bring the man back to life!' I said.

"I touched the man with my staff—the same staff that brought the sheep back to life—and the man came to life. I turned to the old man and asked him if he knew anything about the missing piece of bread.

"'No. I have no knowledge about it at all.'

"We continued on until we came to a very large city. We entered the city and sat down near the gate to rest. I leaned my staff against the wall next to me, fell asleep for a while, and when I woke up noticed that both my staff and the old man were gone! So we wandered around the town looking for my missing staff and the old man.

"In the meantime, the old man, having seen what he thought my staff could do, made his way to the palace of the king. He heard a commotion from the palace and discovered that the king had just been diagnosed with an incurable disease. The court physician had announced there was nothing he could do for the king.

"The old man approached the king and said, 'I have a staff that can cure you of your disease.'

"'If that's true,' said the king, 'I'll give you half my kingdom.'

"The old man was allowed to come closer to the king. With a great display he touched the king with my staff. The king immediately breathed his last and slumped on his bed, dead.

"The old man was straight away hauled off to be hanged, but fortunately for him, this is when my mother and I showed up. I took him down from the scaffold.

"'What do you know about that piece of bread?' I asked.

"He continued to deny knowledge of how it disappeared.

"I must admit, I was very disappointed in this old man, so I asked if I might touch the king with my staff. When given permission, the entire town came to believe in me as a messenger of Allah (most glorious is He)."

The men continue to walk together, but 'Isa is glancing at Jesus to see what impact the story is having on him. They go on at their leisurely pace for a few moments.

"So, let me finish my story," 'Isa begins. "We left the city. The old man, of course, had been shamed by his actions and could not stay. When we were some distance from the city I made three bricks of gold: one for my mother, one for the old man, and one for me. When I gave the old man the gold brick, he broke down and confessed that he had eaten the bread. I gave him my brick, and my mother and I bid him farewell. We continued on our way while he remained behind to savor his good fortune."

Jesus asks, "And what happened to the old man?"

"Apparently, while the old man sat by the roadside with his gold bricks, three robbers happened on him. They killed him and took his bricks.

"The robbers realized how heavy the gold was, so they sent one of their band into town to get some food so they would have the strength to carry these bricks to their cave. The one who went for food put poison in it to kill his companions, but when the man returned with the food, the other two robbers killed him in order to have his share. They then ate the food he brought and promptly died.

"When my mother and I returned the way we had come, we found the dead robbers and the old man where they lay. Thus does the world to her inhabitants."[20]

Jots and Tittles

Al-Maeda 5:48–50

To thee We sent the Scripture in truth confirming the scripture that came before it and guarding it in safety; so judge between them by what Allah hath revealed and follow not their vain desires diverging from the truth that hath come to thee. To each among you have We prescribed a Law and an Open Way. If Allah had so willed He would have made you a single people but (His plan is) to test you in what He hath

Psalm 119:41–48

May your unfailing love come to me, O LORD, your salvation according to your promise; then I will answer the one who taunts me, for I trust in your word.

Do not snatch the word of truth from my mouth, for I have put my hope in your laws. I will always obey your law, for ever and ever.

I will walk about in freedom, for I have sought out your precepts. I will speak of your given you: so strive as in a race in all virtues. The goal of you all is to Allah; it is He that will show you the truth of the matters in which ye dispute.

And this (He commands): Judge thou between them by what Allah hath revealed and follow not their vain desires but beware of them lest they beguile thee from any of that (teaching) which Allah hath sent down to thee. And if they turn away be assured that for some of their crimes it is Allah's purpose to punish them. And truly most men are rebellious.

statutes before kings and will not be put to shame, for I delight in your commands because I love them.

I lift up my hands to your commands, which I love, and I meditate on your decrees.

Unlike the last time Jesus passed by a fig tree with its promise of fruit,[1] the orange tree just ahead has some leftover fruit still clinging to the branches. Seeing the tree with its leftover fruit, they both walk over to it without saying a word.

They stand under the tree, enjoying the juicy fruit with gusto. When they finish, both have orange stains on their sleeves from wiping their mouths. They turn back to the road and begin walking again.

As they pass an empty outbuilding along the road, `Isa, apparently reminded of something, asks, "I mentioned the Torah, Psalms, and Gospel earlier. I noticed that you perked up. Do you remember what I said that got your attention?"

Jesus answers, "Yes, as a matter of fact I do. You said that these books were each a revelation, but the implication was that they were no longer acceptable or were perhaps irrelevant. They had some truth, but not sufficient truth. Did I understand you correctly?"

'Isa says, "That's pretty much it. You see, the Qur'an is the final and complete revelation of Allah (glorious and exalted is He). It confirms and corrects his earlier revelations. It is a book that is truly divine in its beauty, structure and manner of its coming down from our Lord.[2]

"On the other hand," 'Isa continues, "the earlier revelations are no longer complete. Take the Gospel for instance. I was taught by the Lord himself both the Torah and the Gospel.[3] The Gospel, the book given to me by revelation, contained many corrections to the previous revelations."

Jesus looks surprised. He asks, "The Gospel is one book? Where is it? What's in it? And I couldn't help but notice you said it *contained* corrections—past tense."

'Isa is warming to his topic. "Yes, my Gospel was one book. It stands in contradistinction to the four Gospels used by your followers. One book, one message, for Allah is one! Allah sent it down to me in order to confirm the truths still present in the Torah and to correct those human errors that were included in the Torah's text both deliberately and accidentally."[4]

Jesus stops and gently reaches for 'Isa's right arm, then releases it. He is visibly taken aback and says, "You know, those are some incredible claims. How did you come to the conclusion that the Creator reveals his word, allows its corruption, and then reveals another message to take its place or to correct the previous message?"

'Isa begins walking and Jesus joins him. 'Isa replies, "Hmmm . . . I thought everyone knew this. It's widely known and understood. But I have a couple more points for your consideration before we get into that."

Jesus says, "Go ahead, I'm listening."

"As I was saying, the Noble Gospel was just one book and it corrected the previous books. So where the previous revelations were correct, my book confirmed them. And in the places where the older revelations had become corrupted, my Gospel corrected them. Besides, my revelation was full of guidance and light. The Gospel was a book for those who fear Allah (glorious and exalted is He)."

`Isa asks, "Now, about those questions of yours?"

The two have once more stopped walking. At this rate they will never make Jerusalem before dark!

Jesus is carefully thinking about his next statement. He's stroking his chin again. "`Isa, have you considered the wheat fields that surround us? They can help explain one of my problems with what you are suggesting."

`Isa surveys the fields nearly ready for harvest. The wheat is an earthy golden brown, dancing with any wisp of breeze that pushes by.

"How do the wheat fields help?" `Isa asks.

"There was a certain farmer," Jesus begins, "who, in the spring, began to till the soil for his crop. With the benefit of some early spring rains after the farmer sowed his seed, he was pleased to see his seed not only break the ground, but grow quickly. Then the late spring came and the rains ceased. The ripening heads of grain were beginning to droop for lack of water. But his bad fortune didn't stop there. The farmer had to send his son out into the fields to chase away the birds. The young boy also trapped the small animals that were eating the crop. By harvest time the farmer had lost much of his crop, but it was enough to keep his family until the next planting season. This then goes on year after year. The pattern is the same year in and year out."

`Isa looks a bit bewildered.

Jesus explains, "Here's what I mean. The farmer is the prophet of God and the crop is the revelation given to him. The sun, birds, and small animals are the enemies of revelation. First, revelation is sent down to the prophet. With the benefit of some mercy and compassion, the prophet sows his message and watches it spring to life. Then the enemies of God come to ruin the message. The prophet and the people of God are unable to fight off those who would destroy his message. The revelation is slowly eaten away by the lies and corruptions of evil people, with the result that the revelation is unrecognizable. In the end, rather than harvesting for life, the prophet's people are left with a distorted and lie-filled book.

But in the next season a new revelation comes and the situation begins again."

Looking intently at `Isa, Jesus says, "So, you see a pattern of revelation, corruption, and then revelation?" It's really more a statement than a question.

`Isa nods and says, "Yes, absolutely, that's the reality of our situation. Our Lord is most merciful and compassionate to renew his revelation even though it becomes corrupted by liars and evildoers. The pattern is clear. In fact, such a pattern points out the greatness of our Lord, his desire to see that his creation has the right message, and his continual conversation with humanity through his prophets (may the blessings of the Lord rest upon all of them)."

"I think you've understood the pattern," Jesus says, "but missed its significance, `Isa. When my Father is accused of revealing a succession of books that must correct previous books, there are several implications that jump out.

"First," grabbing his left thumb with his right hand, "how is it that a divine word can be altered, manipulated, or changed by any human? Divine revelation is not like a crop of wheat that is affected by rain and sun."

He pauses, then, before `Isa can answer, says, "I suppose the divine word could be spoiled if humans were more powerful than the Creator." He says this with a mischievous smile.

Now with a slight shrug, Jesus continues, "No, the word of the Lord is eternal. It is settled forever.[5] Don't you see that a word from the Creator is by definition an eternal word, a message that is unchangeable? If it is otherwise, it cannot be from the Almighty. That's like trying to accept the possibility of a square circle or a . . ."

`Isa jumps in. "Or a friendly camel?"

There is a hearty chuckle from both men. Jesus continues, "Yes, a friendly camel! So, you do understand."

`Isa begins walking again. Jesus joins him. `Isa says, "What I understand is that our Lord is most merciful. He has promised that his final revelation, the Holy Qur'an revealed to Prophet Muhammad, will in no wise suffer the alterations of all previous revelations. He himself guarantees its everlasting purity.[6] He never vouchsafed his earlier messages."[7]

Jesus responds, "I understand what you are saying, but I believe this pattern of revelation and corruption dishonors the very character of my heavenly Father. Such a pattern shows us he is not compassionate as much as he's just plain sloppy. This constant repetition of sending a message, waiting for corruption, and then resending the message does not speak of a merciful God but, at worst, his inability to prevent corruption and, at best, an indifference to the alteration of his message—a message humans depend on in order to know and obey the commands of the Lord."

Passing before them is an old man. He is leading a wretched-looking boney donkey pulling an even sicklier-looking cart. Neither Jesus nor `Isa seem to notice.

Jesus continues, "And if such a pattern reveals that we can't trust the Father to keep his word and message free from error, isn't this the same as admitting that the Almighty, rather than protecting his revelation, has willingly condemned to the hellfire those who unwittingly trusted a corrupted message?"

`Isa gives a knowing nod. "Jesus, your point is valid if you begin with your assumption."

"And what assumption was that?"

"You presume," `Isa answers, "that our Lord is somehow obligated to a defined set of rules. You assume that our Lord (glorious and exalted is He) must conform himself to our needs, to our wants, to that which he has created. You are making the created greater than the Creator."

Jesus is looking at his hand, rubbing one of those welts he received at his crucifixion. "You learned Torah from your Lord, did you not?"

"Yes!" `Isa exclaims. "Allah said, 'Behold! I taught thee the Book and Wisdom the Law and the Gospel.'"[8]

"Why would your Lord give you a corrupted book from which to learn?"

`Isa chuckles. "Oh, but he didn't. He didn't give me the corrupted book of the Jews, but the book that resides in heaven, the Mother of all books, a Tablet Preserved."[9]

Jesus asks, "But doesn't the same Tablet Preserved contain the Torah, Psalms, and Gospel?"

"Of course! How else could I have learned the uncorrupted version?" `Isa responds.

Again Jesus asks, "So, God has preserved his word—including the earlier books—for eternity in heaven. He just hasn't kept them pure among humanity?"

`Isa nods his head, "Yes."

Jesus says, "I don't understand why my disciples are commanded in the book of Muhammad to hold fast to these previous revelations if they are tainted with lies and the words of men. Certainly, your Lord must have stated very clearly in your Holy Book that the books of Moses and David, and my book, too, are not worthy of our attention since they are corrupted."

`Isa replies, "I'm surprised, Jesus. Don't you know that our people changed the words of our Scriptures from their right times and places?[10] They actually pretended obedience and loyalty to the word of our Lord, but, in the end, they distorted it."

"I agree," Jesus replies. "In the past our fathers did not always deal honestly with our law. As the Holy Scripture says, they changed the words. The prophet Jeremiah speaks of lying scribes,[11] and we both know there are many of our teachers who misapply the text, thereby distorting the meaning. So, when the scribes and rabbis falsify the context of a certain passage, the message is lost.[12] But hiding the meaning in an oral presentation is far different from actually changing or altering the text, isn't it?"

"It was our Lord," `Isa begins, "who revealed the law. It was a guide to the lost. It was a light in the darkness. But Allah gave responsibility for the law to the rabbis and doctors of the law. They were supposed to protect it, but instead, they ended up selling it to any who would pay the price. They should not be considered as servants of Allah, but unbelievers!"[13]

Jesus nods and asks, "Again, did the rabbis actually change the text, or, according to you, were they chided for writing their own words and calling it Scripture? And, if I may be so bold as to respectfully disagree with you on one point: it was not the rabbis and doctors of the law who were to preserve the book. That responsibility belongs to my Father. Who else has the ability to take on such a task? It is impossible for any human to preserve the divine. Do we ask the child to feed his mother?"

Jesus recites in Hebrew: "Your word I have treasured in my heart that I may not sin against You."[14] He translates the verse for `Isa and then continues, "I know you'll agree that only the Holy One can perfectly and ultimately preserve his word. After all, why else would you believe in a Preserved Tablet? But there are countless numbers of my followers who have hidden the word of the Lord in their hearts. That is, they have memorized large portions of the text, thus helping to preserve the integrity of the divine message."[15]

`Isa replies, "Yes, I agree. Putting the Lord's words in our hearts is a righteous act. The Book of Allah is an inheritance for the servants of Allah.[16] Further, Allah (glorious and exalted is He) has indeed kept his book pure. And the proof that he has done this is that the Qur'an memorized by the disciples of Prophet Muhammad (the peace and blessings of our Lord be upon him) will be the very same Qur'an memorized by his disciples in every century after him."

Jesus responds, "`Isa, it seems to me we're saying pretty much the same thing about the books of my followers and of yours. Both are covered with a divine protection. Both are memorized and held within the hearts of our disciples. Doesn't the Qur'an agree that the revelations given to Moses, to David, and to me were just that—revelations from God?"[17]

The road continues to rise and fall with the landscape. The sun's intensity is seen in the moisture on `Isa's face. Both see an approaching well, perhaps twenty cubits off the road. With silent assent, the two make for the well.

A young girl, about ten, is drawing water and pouring it into a clay jar that seems too large for her tiny frame. She has a coiled piece of cloth sitting on the side of the well, ready to place on her head in order to cushion the heavy water jar.

Smiling, Jesus greets her. "Shalom, young lady. Could we trouble you for some water for two thirsty travelers?"

"Yes, sir," she replies. The girl is small, but strong for her age. She is barefoot. Her clothes are dirty. Her eyes are bright, though her face is smudged with dirt. She has been getting the water for her family for a few years now, several times a day. Every movement is sure and confident, and she wastes no energy bringing up more water. Refilling her smaller jar for the men, she hands it to Jesus. He offers it to `Isa, who declines. Jesus drinks from the jar, water dribbling down his chin and onto his tunic. He again offers the jar to `Isa. He now takes it, slaking his thirst.

Handing the jar back to the girl, `Isa says, "What is your name, young lady?"

"Elizabeth, sir," she answers. She hardly looks the men in the eyes, but keeps her head bowed. Her parents have taught her well.

"Elizabeth," `Isa repeats. "Well, Elizabeth, please inform your father that he has a daughter who is well mannered and a credit to her family."

She blushes slightly. "Thank you, sir."

As `Isa and Jesus turn and move back to the road, the girl is curiously trying to steal glimpses of the two men without their notice.

Jesus asks, "`Isa, can we get back to the Gospel you were given? I have a couple of questions."

"As you wish."

"You say it was one Gospel. What was in it? Where is it now?"

`Isa answers, "The Gospel revealed to me confirmed the message of the Holy Qur'an—that there is one Lord. All the previous books were corrected by my Gospel."

"But where is that Gospel now?" Jesus asks. "Do your disciples have it?"

Again `Isa responds, "It is lost. No one knows where it is. The details behind its loss are not relevant. What matters most is that the Holy Qur'an is the final book of Allah."

Jesus again queries, "But surely some fragment or scrap must still survive?"

`Isa answers as if he has answered this question many times, almost sighing as he speaks. "The evidence that matters about the existence of my Gospel is found in the Qur'an. No other evidence is necessary."

"All right," Jesus says. "I must accept the absence of your Gospel as prescribed in the Qur'an. So let me ask. Didn't it contain stories arranged in such a way as to show the purpose in your coming, the stories you told, the message you preached, the people you healed, your influence on the culture, and ultimately your death at the cross?"

You can hear `Isa inhale, as if slightly indignant. "Nothing remains of the book. All that is necessary is the Qur'an, or else Allah (glorious and exalted is He) would have saved the book for humanity."

Jesus begins speaking excitedly now and by so doing his walking pace also begins to pick up. "So, your disciples do not have your biography except what is found in the book brought by Muhammad?"

`Isa nods, "But what they have is sufficient. The message of our Lord is not about me, but about him."

Jesus shakes his head and *tsks-tsks* his tongue. "That's indeed a great loss. My followers have a very full, though hardly complete, accounting of all that I began to do and to teach.[18] My message is that the Creator sent me in order to establish his kingdom among his people. This kingdom is here now, right here among my disciples.[19] As I said earlier, the miracles I performed and the healings I did all pointed to the presence of the kingdom, the sovereign rule of my Father.[20]

"Unlike you, `Isa, I did not come to correct the previous revelations. No, I came to fulfill them,[21] for they spoke of the day when the people of God would be rescued from the Evil One, from judgment and death, and brought out of exile. And just as in the previous Scriptures, the key operative is faith. You know, trust and reliance in the character and promises of my Father.[22]

"So, my coming is in order to keep divine promises, promises to Adam, Noah, Abraham, Isaac, Jacob, Judah, and all those who will have the hardness of their hearts removed and replaced with a new heart."[23]

Jesus pauses, takes a breath, and finishes his thoughts: "No, my Gospel is not necessary because the previous messages are corrupted. In fact, it's just the opposite. My Gospel is necessary because the previous books are true!"

`Isa is thinking about what Jesus has said. He grins and says, "I'll admit that's a nice turn of phrase there . . . but it doesn't alter the fact that my Gospel is one book, my message is one message, and my Lord is one."

`Isa then asks, "So, what's with your followers and four Gospels? How is it helpful to have four distinct messages that contradict each other when the desired goal is one message about our Lord?"

Jesus shrugs. "The camel has four legs, but still runs in the same direction."

The beginnings of a grin appear on `Isa's face. "You certainly like stories and proverbs, don't you?"

"Sure, don't you? Don't you use them both to clarify and to obfuscate your teaching? Wait, your Gospel doesn't exist, so there is no way to know how or what you taught, right?"

`Isa's grin disappears and he reiterates, "The Qur'an is the final message from our Lord. It is complete, without error and without addition. My message is one and the same as the Qur'an."

They walk on for a few minutes, taking in the fields, the sky, the birds. Then `Isa adds, "Look at that." He is pointing to a group of four young boys playing just off the road among the olive trees.

He says, "Let's go see what they're doing."

Boys with Beetles

Al-i-Imran 3:49

And (appoint him) an Apostle to the Children of Israel (with this message): I have come to you with a sign from your Lord in that I make for you out of clay as it were the figure of a bird and breathe into it and it becomes a bird by Allah's leave; and I heal those born blind and the lepers and I quicken the dead by Allah's leave; and I declare to you what ye eat and what ye store in your houses.

Luke 2:41–52

Every year his parents went to Jerusalem for the Feast of the Passover. When he was twelve years old, they went up to the Feast, according to the custom. After the Feast was over, while his parents were returning home, the boy Jesus stayed behind in Jerusalem, but they were unaware of it. Thinking he was in their company, they traveled on for a day. Then they began looking for him among their relatives and friends. When they

Surely therein is a Sign for you if ye did believe.

did not find him, they went back to Jerusalem to look for him.

After three days they found him in the temple courts, sitting among the teachers, listening to them and asking them questions. Everyone who heard him was amazed at his understanding and his answers.

When his parents saw him, they were astonished. His mother said to him, "Son, why have you treated us like this? Your father and I have been anxiously searching for you."

"Why were you searching for me?" he asked. "Didn't you know I had to be in my Father's house?"

But they did not understand what he was saying to them. Then he went down to Nazareth with them and was obedient to them. But his mother treasured all these things in her heart. And Jesus grew in wisdom and stature, and in favor with God and men.

The four boys are not any older than seven or eight. Each is a bit of a ragamuffin: scrawny, dirty, barefoot, dark flashing eyes, brilliant smiles. There is an effervescent buoyancy and exhilaration in their voices, as if they have discovered something for the first time.

'Isa and Jesus are drawing closer, working their way through the olive trees. The boys don't seem to be paying attention to them because whatever has their interest is so much more engrossing.

The four are all crouching on their knees in a circle. Their hands are busy with something. The two men are still not close enough to see exactly what it is, but the boys are abuzz with energy and excitement for their project.

'Isa and Jesus finally stand over the circle of boys. One of the boys looks up and notices them, but quickly returns his efforts to his work. The four have captured four big beetles, the type that is often found during the spring. The boys are in the process of trying to tie lengths of cord to one leg of each beetle. Their hands are a whirr as they attempt to hold a buzzing beetle, tie the cord, and then—with frustrating sighs as their prey escapes—attempt it all over again.

'Isa and Jesus look at each other, smiling, as if they both have the same memory from their childhoods. After a few minutes of watching the boys, Jesus says, "Mighty men of valor, my congratulations on your successful capture of these honorable foes!" The boys barely notice.

'Isa remarks, "Ah, the wonders of youth. Come on, Jesus, we should get going. Remember, the dog may bark, but the caravan moves on."

As they turn to work their way back to the road, one of the boys shouts with glee, "I did it. It's flying. Look, Shlomo, it's flying."

Jesus and 'Isa turn around. The boy is standing with the cord in his right hand. The beetle is furiously buzzing, trying to escape its captor, but to no avail. The more it struggles and attempts to fly away, the happier and louder grow the shouts of the boys. Soon, the other three have successfully corded their mighty flying beasts, erupting with shouts of joy and amazement as each of the beetles zig-zaggedly attempts to escape from each leaping and excited little boy.

Jesus looks from the boys to 'Isa and says, "'Isa, the dog may bark and the caravan moves on, but if a boy has a beetle, he cares nothing for the caravan."

Ducking through the low growth of the trees, the two men are now at the road's edge. They turn up the road and their long journey continues.

`Isa says wistfully, "A boy and his beetle, a great joy to behold. You know, I'm reminded of my own childhood. I remember one day when I was playing with some friends. We were making lots of animals from the moistened dirt—well, clay, really. There was lots of noise and commotion as we played with our animals. I took a couple of handfuls of the clay and began to fashion a bird. I don't remember which type I was trying to make. Perhaps it was just, you know, the general idea of a bird.

"Well, anyway, I made several birds. As I finished each one I set it on the ground in a line, as if ready to start a race. When I had finished fashioning my fine flock, I'm not sure what came over me, but somehow I knew that I had the permission of the Lord (glorious and exalted is He). I blew over my newly formed flock of clay birds, and with my breath each clay bird became a real bird, feathers, beak, and all! Each flew away to join others of its kind."

Jesus' eyes brighten as he listens to the story.

`Isa continues, "My friends hadn't really been paying attention to what I was doing, since we were all busy making something from the dirt. But when those birds came to life, my friends certainly did take notice. They were dumbstruck." `Isa shrugs. "Well, who wouldn't be?"

Jesus marvels, "`Isa, that's quite a story. I wish I'd been there to witness it. I can imagine the looks on the faces of your friends—real birds from clay. That's something!

"I never did anything like that as a child," Jesus says. "I do know, however, that my followers will fabricate stories about my childhood."

`Isa interrupts, "So you admit your people make up stories about you. That is just what the Holy Qur'an says will happen. On the last day, Allah (most glorious is He) will raise me to himself and clear my name of all the lies people have told about me."[1]

"Wait just a second," Jesus responds, "I'm not speaking about the stories found in the Gospels, but stories that will come much later, that are make-believe. The real truth about my life is found in the four Gospels. These will have selected and focused stories about my life and ministry. These four books won't be a simple running commentary or narrative that covers every moment of my life. Each author's purpose will be revealed in the stories he selects from my life.

"There will be, of course, one or two stories of my childhood in the Gospels. But this will leave my followers wondering, 'What happened to Jesus when he was a young boy? Did he know he was the Messiah? Did he know the powers he had? Was he aware of his purpose in life at a young age? How exactly did his family escape from King Herod? What happened to his father?' and so forth. These questions will lead my followers to create stories. They will have good intentions, naturally, and the stories will answer these questions. The problem with such stories is that they are just that—stories. Made-up, fanciful, imaginative tales."

`Isa nods his head in agreement, "Yes, I know what you mean. The Holy Qur'an has very little of my life in its pages. It's mostly just my birth, my sayings, and where I fit into the plans of our Lord."

Jesus touches his nose with a sly grin and asks, "So, the story you just told about the birds coming to life, that's in the Qur'an, is it?"

"Yes, it's the only story of my childhood, except for my birth, that's in the Holy Book."

Jesus says, "I find that rather amusing."

`Isa agrees. "Yes, the story has a certain kind of humor to it, I suppose."

"Well," Jesus replies, extending the word in a sing-song manner. "I didn't mean the story itself as much as the idea of the story's being one of the few stories about you in your book, considering where it comes from."

`Isa has that "here we go again" look. "All right, I know what you mean. You're going to say the origin of the story isn't the Holy Book of Allah, but some pre-qur'anic Jewish or Christian source, right?"[2]

Jesus grins slyly again. "He who has ears to hear, let him hear."

`Isa says, "Does the gosling teach the goose to swim?"

Jesus stops, turns toward `Isa and says, "I have a story to tell you."

Taking up his stride again, Jesus begins. "It was a custom for my family to go up to Jerusalem for the Passover. It was the highlight of the year for us. We prepared, planned, and packed for it pretty much the day after we returned home from the previous Passover.

"Finally, the day would arrive for us to join the caravan bound for Jerusalem. We attached ourselves to a group of pilgrims with their donkeys burdened with pots, sacks, and sometimes even a pregnant woman. There were wobbly camels who could carry an entire household of goods, but whose temperament was closer to a typhoon than these gentle spring rains we've been having. Young and old, men and women, all walking, often singing the praises of Jerusalem or just telling stories of past journeys to Jerusalem for Passover. I think of those times with great fondness. Even now as we approach Jerusalem, I can't help but think about the smells of that trip, the sounds—the tinkling bells around the necks of the camels, the jabbering of the little kids playing games as they walked, the occasional outbursts of song, the theological discussions of the old men, and even the chatter of some of the wives. It was all music to my ears.

"I remember especially one of these trips. I was twelve years old and this was my first Passover as a son of the Torah. I was happy to wear the phylactery as a badge of my maturity and relationship to the Almighty. And it was an especially happy occasion, since my mother had chosen to come along this time.

"We walked a long time and finally reached Jerusalem. I saw the temple as if for the first time: the house of my Father. Of course, the events of Passover are always special, and at this Passover they became very meaningful to me. There was always inside me a small ambling creek of awareness—an awareness of who the Almighty is and who I am with relation to him—and then on this trip it suddenly becomes a rushing river of awareness."

Jesus pauses. His voice has a small tremble in it. "This awareness, this feeling of knowing who I am and why I am here had somehow intensified.

"Well, in Jerusalem we performed the ritual of Passover. There was the wonder of the wine, the breaking of the bread, dipping the bitter herbs into salt water, and that lamb, the wonderful roasted lamb that we ate."

He pauses again and closes his eyes as if reliving every moment. "Ahh, what a marvelous picture of my people's exit from the land of Egypt."

`Isa is nodding, enjoying the story.

Jesus says, "It's also a rich symbol for God's people, true Israel, leaving the kingdom of darkness for God's kingdom of light. I really understood the temple to be the house of my Father and this ritual, the Passover, was the symbol of freedom and forgiveness.

"Well, when we had kept the seven days of Passover, it was time to pack up the family, gather the animals, and meet up with the caravan that was headed back to Nazareth. My family found the right caravan and off they went. They traveled for a full day before they knew something was amiss.

"Later my mother would tell me, 'We didn't miss you at first because we figured you were with Aunt Elizabeth or your Uncle Ephraim. So we didn't panic. We knew you were safe with them. But when the caravan stopped for the night and you didn't come to our camp, I was worried to tears.'

"My parents and some other relatives feverishly searched the caravan for me. They asked all their friends, relatives, and anyone they knew even slightly. My mother told me she was a total wreck when they discovered I wasn't anywhere among the caravan.

"My parents did the only thing they could do: they left the caravan and returned to Jerusalem. When they arrived they searched everywhere. They went back to our lodgings. They scoured the market. They must have turned over every rock. Finally, in an act of desperation, they went back to the temple. And it was there they found me. I was on the terrace where the members of the Sanhedrin address the people on the Sabbath or on feast days."

Again, Jesus' infectious grin appears.

"Yes, there I was, a twelve-year-old boy engaged with the learned men of Torah, priests and scribes. We all sat together in kind of a semicircle."

Jesus abruptly stops his story and asks `Isa, "Do you know what was so unique about that experience?"

"No, what?" `Isa asks.

"It was as if I belonged there, as if I'd found my place in the world, right there in the temple."

`Isa nods and intones, "Hmm."

Jesus asks, "Have you ever had the feeling that you were doing the very thing you are here for? Ever felt like the very thing you're doing and the words you're speaking are exactly right?"

`Isa nods his head vigorously, "Sure!"

"Well, that's precisely how it was. It was a wonderful feeling."

His tone changes from the wistful to the serious.

"Of course," Jesus says, "my parents weren't delighted! When they saw me, they didn't come rushing over right away. I think they were a bit stunned. They watched and listened for some time. They observed that I was both listening intently and asking insightful questions. But they also heard me answer the questions posed by the teachers of Torah. Did I say they were stunned? That's an understatement. They were nonplussed! They'd never seen or heard anything like this before."

Jesus smiles at the other man as he recounts the experience: "But . . . my mom was still my mother. When she finally overcame her amazement, she walked up to the circle of men with her hands on her hips like this." Jesus demonstrates it.

"And then she said, 'My child, why did you treat us like this? Your father and I have been looking for you everywhere.'

"I chuckled a bit because my mother called me a child—her little boy—but obviously she did that because she had been worried about me and was now slightly miffed to see that I was fine, that I wasn't lost, scared, or lonely. In fact, I was better than fine. I was having the time of my life.

"But I didn't say any of that to her. As amazed as they were at discovering me in the temple, I was equally amazed they would think I'd be somewhere else! 'How is it you would think I'd be anywhere else?' I asked.

"Then I calmly added, 'You knew it was necessary for me to be about the things of my Father.'"

`Isa wrinkles his brow and asks, "I thought you said your father was a carpenter. What business does a carpenter have in the temple with the scholars of the law? And this is the third time you've mentioned the temple as your father's house."

Jesus answers, "Good point. In fact, my parents were confused about it as well. Let me just say this: it was from this day onward that I began the process of coming to an understanding, having a developing awareness within me that my purpose for being here was not to make clay birds come to life . . ."

`Isa's face shadows and his brow furrows. "What I did as a child I did by the permission of Allah (glorious and exalted is He). It was no parlor trick. It revealed to the people that I was a sign, a prophet, an example, and one who was to be given a book."

"Sorry, `Isa. I meant no disrespect," Jesus quickly interjects. "I only meant to say that anyone who follows my life as revealed in Holy Scripture sees a gradual awareness of my own understanding of my vocation, my purpose, my reason for being here. I didn't mean to say that your story doesn't do the same. It's just that the stories that are told about me are intricately linked. They all show who I am and why I came. I'm not sure the stories in your Scriptures unfold the same message about you as my Scriptures reveal about me."

`Isa asks, "Well, what do you mean by 'more intricately linked'?"

"Funny you should ask. Just the other day I was sharing with my disciples on this very road." He is looking at the ground and motioning to the road with both hands. "I reminded them of the necessity that the Messiah suffer and die according to Moses, the Prophets, and the entire Book of God."

`Isa jumps in. "Wait, wait, wait! The Messiah doesn't die on a cross. I was not crucified! You can't be the Messiah if you die on a cross. It's dishonoring to our Lord. I am a prophet of Allah. A prophet would not die with such ignominy and shame."

The corners of Jesus' mouth rise slightly. "Yes, I know, but let's put off that topic for a few minutes. Let me show you that the stories in the

Book of God are connected. They give the hearer and reader the proper understanding of who I am."

`Isa says, "Yes, go ahead. We'll come back to this idea of the so-called crucifixion."

The road is winding through another nearby olive orchard. The trees are gnarled and twisted with age, having given their owner many good years of olive oil. A slight breeze rustles their boughs and leaves, making the trees whisper their soothing spring song.

"The first thing," Jesus states, "is that I began to sense my calling, my vocation, what my Father had sent me to do. This began on that Passover of my twelfth year. When we returned to Nazareth I grew not only physically, but also in terms of wisdom and in grace with God and people.

"The next event that reveals my growing awareness of being Messiah was my baptism by my cousin John in the Jordan River."[3]

"Baptism?" `Isa asks. "You were baptized? What on earth for?"

Jesus answers, "It was necessary because as I rose from the swirling water, I heard my Father say, 'You are my beloved son. I am very pleased with you.' This was my Father confirming my growing awareness of messiahship. The house of my Father gave me the sense of being in the right place, and being called the Son of the Father confirmed my relationship to him."

Jesus senses another question from `Isa, but quickly says, "Wait, there's more. I was made strong by God's Spirit and entered into a test with the Evil One. During my days with the Tempter, even he recognized me as the Son of God.[4] Being God's Son means I have a mission. I have a purpose. I have a unique ministry that must be accomplished for the glory of the Creator."

`Isa asks wearily, "And what is that mission? You know, Jesus, I never did any of this. This is all so dramatic that . . . well, it's so dramatic that I have to doubt it. Why all the theatrics?"

Jesus gives an understanding nod and says, "It may be dramatic, but that doesn't make it fiction. In fact, the stories my followers will tell about me carry so much authenticity and contextual accuracy, the only doubt raised is why people *don't* believe them.

"You know, those days in the wilderness of Satan were difficult. I was in the desert for forty days and forty nights. The desert day is difficult enough, but the nights are more so. Wild animals, strange sounds, the cold, the wind—I have to tell you it was a very difficult time for me. I was sorely tempted by the Father of Lies to try out my powers just to keep my sanity. But in the end, it was the word of God that rescued me. That time in the desert helped me see the struggle with what it means to be Messiah."

`Isa is listening, but he is saying nothing and seems detached. Either he has never heard anything like this before or he thinks Jesus is loony.

"Anyway," Jesus continues, "I was invited to speak in my hometown synagogue.[5] I read from the prophet of Isaiah: 'The spirit of the Lord is upon me, because he anointed me; to preach the gospel to the poor he has sent me, to proclaim release to the captives, and to the blind new sight, to send forth the broken in release, to proclaim the Lord's acceptable year.'[6]

"`Isa, did you hear it? I'm the Anointed One. This anointing comes from God's Spirit. I am here to preach the Lord's acceptable year: forgiveness, freedom, and the kingdom. This is what the Son of God does. These are the things he preaches. The people he frees and heals and gives sight to and releases are those who have such great need!

"My time with Satan helped me see the potential of my calling. My sermon gave me the opportunity to express how I would implement these powers. You see, these are the kinds of stories you find in the Gospels. They are stories intricately linked and interrelated to help the hearer understand who I am. Your book doesn't do this, does it?"

Both men have now stopped again. Jesus stands looking at `Isa, waiting for his response. They have finally passed through the olive trees. `Isa is looking at the hills to his right. They are far away, verdant, inviting.

And then turning, he looks intently at Jesus. "Is this man mad?" he wonders. "How could anyone be the Son of God?"

After a few moments of wondering, rationality catches up with him.

`Isa says, "I understand all that you've said, Jesus. It even makes sense in a strange way. Don't get me wrong. I don't agree with your conclusions, but I do see what you're saying. Ultimately, I must also remind you that the Gospel came to and was acted on by the People of the Book[7] until the Qur'an comes to take its place."[8]

Jesus smiles. "A story is not without honor except in its hometown, I guess."

`Isa smiles, too, and says, "So now you need to explain how it is you were crucified. I have the feeling this is something we both have strong feelings about."

Jesus says, "You're right. So let's agree to disagree amicably."

Did He or Didn't He Die?

An-Nisa 4:157–58

That they said (in boast) "We killed Christ Jesus the son of Mary the Apostle of Allah"; but they killed him not nor crucified him but so it was made to appear to them and those who differ therein are full of doubts with no (certain) knowledge but only conjecture to follow for of a surety they killed him not.

Nay Allah raised him up unto Himself; and Allah is Exalted in Power Wise.

Luke 23:44–46, 50–53

It was now about the sixth hour, and darkness came over the whole land until the ninth hour, for the sun stopped shining. And the curtain of the temple was torn in two.

Jesus called out with a loud voice, "Father, into your hands I commit my spirit." When he had said this, he breathed his last. . . .

Now there was a man named Joseph, . . . of Arimathea. . . . Going to Pilate, he asked

And there is none of the People of the Book but must believe in him before his death; and on the Day of Judgment He will be a witness against them. ■

for Jesus' body. Then he took it down, wrapped it in linen cloth and placed it in a tomb cut in the rock, one in which no one had yet been laid. ■

The men have now walked about half the distance to Jerusalem. It has taken them considerably longer than if either had been by himself. There have been some moments to rest, moments for observation, and times of intense discussion. The conversation is going to move to a new level of intensity with the argument for Jesus' crucifixion—and for `Isa's non-crucifixion.

The road to Jerusalem is less uphill now, but has plateaued. The men confidently stride toward the city that symbolizes much of their ministries.

`Isa says, "You gave an interesting narrative that allegedly links one story to the next with the aim of providing reasons for your ministry. I'd like to do the same to show you the Qur'an is not lacking in literary value! First, our Lord says that I was born, I will die, and I will be raised up."[1]

Jesus interrupts, "Wait. So you are crucified. Your believers will initially understand that this is a reference to your death on the cross, right?"

`Isa quickly replies, "Yes and no. The 'yes' is that my followers initially understood the revelation to mean I was raised from the dead—"

Jesus interrupts again. "But wait. Even your book says that someone died on the cross. Your book confirms the fact of a crucifixion, doesn't it?"

"Wait now, I'm not finished," `Isa replies. "I've already given you the 'yes,' but there's a 'no,' too. In the same chapter that says I will be raised to life is a nearly identical verse about John. He will be born, he will die, and he will be raised to life again.[2] The raising to life of John means that in the last hour when every person is resurrected, he also will be resurrected.[3] This applies equally to me. I will be raised to life on the Day of Judgment, and not until."

Jesus looks incredulous. "But to be raised to life implies that one must first die, doesn't it?"

`Isa answers, "That's right, and it will please Allah to kill me before he does that."

Jesus takes a sharp breath at this statement. "So, it is ignominy to have one of the Lord's prophets die at the hands of human beings, but a different matter if God takes his life?"

"That's right," `Isa agrees.

Jesus seems at a loss for words.

Then `Isa continues, "Now, let me bring some light to your assumption that someone else died on the cross. The Jews will boast, 'We killed Christ, the son of Mary.' But our Lord says, 'They did not kill him.' That's right, Jesus. I was not crucified. It was only made to appear that this was the case. The result is that there is much confusion and doubt about the whole event.

"Now let me go through this slowly. I want to make this very clear. First, the Jews desired to kill me. Previously, they had broken the covenant with our Lord. My people were little more than blasphemers.[4] They rejected faith and even libeled my mother with a false charge.[5]

"Second, the Jews boasted they had succeeded with their plot. They thought they'd killed me, but our Lord is most clear. He says it was made to appear this way to them."

Jesus adds, "So, someone replaced you on the cross?"

`Isa responds immediately, "No, that's not what Allah (most glorious is He) says. I realize that is how many folks interpret the verse, including many of my followers, but why make the words say more than they really say?

"I know some will suggest that I was on the cross, but did not die. Others will offer that I died on the cross, but that the death I suffered was only in the body. Allah also says of the martyrs, for instance, 'They are living though you do not see it.'"[6]

With a deliberate snap of his fingers, `Isa almost barks, "My point is that what you have heard are merely interpretations. They are not faithful to the words of Allah (glorious and exalted is He)!

"Third, remember that the Lord says there are many doubts and that no one has sure knowledge about the event."

Jesus still has an amazed and doubtful look on his face, but he is listening. He nods for `Isa to continue.

`Isa says, "Who are these people who differ with the truth? They are ones who say I was crucified. They don't have certain knowledge. They're left with conjectures. They have doubts. Their doubts don't pertain to the question of who was on the cross, but rather to what they know—or think they know.

Jesus says, "So . . ."

`Isa jumps in and says, "Wait, let me finish this sequence of revelations. I think it will answer some of your objections.

"In another revelation, later still, Allah (glorious and exalted is He) will say to me, ``Isa, I will take you and raise you to myself. I myself will clear you of all false charges. Those who follow you will be superior to those who reject true religion.'"

`Isa looks intently at Jesus and says, "The Lord of the Universe will then resurrect all people and, further, he will judge every matter that people argue about.[7]

"When Allah says he 'will take' me it means he will cause me to die, but as I said earlier this all takes place on the day of resurrection.

"Furthermore, Allah has the power to destroy me, the Messiah, if he wishes. Don't you agree that our Lord has the power, if he wishes, to destroy me, the son of Maryam, and everyone else on the earth?"[8]

With that, `Isa crosses his arms on his chest. His last question is less of a question and more of a declaration. He seems quite confident now.

Jesus says nothing, but closely observes `Isa.

"Jesus, it's clear that I'm the Messiah, and what's more, I didn't face death on a cross. I will die before the last hour and then be resurrected. My death, especially on a cross, would shame the Lord."

Jesus doesn't respond but continues walking. He is thinking about all that he is hearing from `Isa. It is certainly a different take on the life and death of the Messiah than what he has experienced.

Just then, two small dogs appear from behind the two men. One is mostly black and the other beige with white spots on its face and right front paw. They are scraggly, looking hungry, but obviously belong to a nearby farmer. These dogs look as if they could chase down a rabbit quite easily. The beige dog is friendly and nuzzles first Jesus' leg, then `Isa's. Jesus is about to reach down to pet the dog when he sees `Isa's reaction. `Isa is not afraid, but seems very uneasy, as if he knew contact with the poor beast would give him an incurable disease. `Isa does not reach down for the dog. He stands still, hoping the dogs will go away.[9]

"Shoo now, boys," Jesus waves his hands at the dogs. They take the hint and scamper off into the fields that line the road.

`Isa repeats the last statement from his monologue in order to jump-start the conversation, as if the dogs had never been there. "My death would most certainly shame our Lord. Don't you agree?"

Surprisingly, Jesus says, "I do agree. If you are not the Messiah, and I am, then your death on the cross would indeed be for nothing. It would have been in vain."

From the look on his face, this is apparently not the answer `Isa was expecting.

Jesus states, "So I guess here's the rub: we are very different in how we perceive our ministries. You are first and foremost an example, the apostle to the Jews, an announcer of Ahmad, a preacher of the oneness of God.

"I, on the other hand, come announcing the kingdom of God, bringing freedom to the captives and offering forgiveness to those who repent. This forgiveness, this freedom and liberty, all comes with a cost. My death on the cross was that price. My death on the cross bought and paid for the sins of many."

`Isa pulls at his earlobe and says, "Yes, we're very different in our perceptions."

"You know that if you did not die on the cross," Jesus offers, "you most certainly did not rise from the dead on the third day."

"Yes," `Isa agrees. "That seems pretty obvious. Since I was not crucified, I was not in the tomb."

"And if you did not rise from the dead," Jesus continues, "you could not have submitted yourself to the will of the Father. By submitting—"

`Isa interrupts. "But I *am* submitted to Allah!"

Jesus raises both hands, palms facing `Isa, as if to reassure him. "I know, but on the one hand, your submission simply provides your followers an example, and a worthy one at that. On the other hand, when I submit myself to my Father's will, I am able to restore men and women to their rightful place as his children. I give my Father's children back the position of power they had before they sinned, and I give them my innocence where they had broken the command of God. You see, `Isa, all this and more besides was achieved by my going to the cross."

`Isa objects, "But death by crucifixion was not necessary to accomplish any of that. All a person has to do is look to Allah, repent, and trust in his mercy and compassion. Allah is compassionate and most merciful.[10] Allah simply forgives. Your death, I'm afraid, Jesus, was in vain!"

Jesus swats away a fly buzzing around his head. "Not in vain, not at all. It might've been for nothing if it hadn't originated with my Father, but the Father did send me for the explicit purpose of suffering, dying, and rising from the grave as a ransom for many.

"You know, `Isa, I didn't come as just another prophet bringing the exact same message as the previous prophets."[11]

Jesus sees a restlessness rising up in `Isa. "No, I'm not saying I have a new or contradictory message," Jesus says. "May God forbid! What I mean is that the work of Moses and all the prophets was building toward my coming, my crucifixion, and my resurrection."

"What?" `Isa exclaims. "What are you talking about?"

"I thought you'd never ask! Let me ask you this question: Is God's revelation cyclical, or does it point the people of God to some important future event?"

"It seems to me," `Isa muses, "that your question is rhetorical! I guess you're going to make the case that the revelation somehow points to the future?"

"Before I do," Jesus says, "think about your own ministry. You've already said you came as another of many biblical prophets. Their message is yours: God is one and we must submit to him. This sounds rather cyclical and repetitive, as opposed to the Scriptures that are familiar to me."

`Isa says, "All right, while I may not fully agree, I see your point."

"Good. Then let me show you how the story my Father has laid out in his revelation points to something that was to happen.

"From the very beginning, that is, with Adam and Eve, my Father has desired relationship with us—intimacy with us. That is why he walked in the garden with our first parents. That is why he was with his people as they came out of slavery from Egypt. Moses tells us the Lord came down on Mt. Sinai in the sight of all the people.[12] He even gave the people visible proof of his presence with them: the fire by night and the cloud of glory by day.

"`Isa, you mentioned Moses as the prophet to be compared with another later prophet. Well, what made Moses so great, if not the fact that he spoke with God, met with God, and reflected his glory?

"This is how I would summarize these early stories of the Holy Scriptures: people cannot go to heaven to meet God. Rather, God comes to earth to meet and be with them.

"But the sad thing is that after this, most of the Scriptures show how humanity rebuffed God's efforts to draw close to them. There is the golden calf episode that results in punishment. There is the reluctance to enter the Promised Land and the limited obedience of the people, resulting in limited blessing. And for the next many generations, the people of Israel remain at an arm's distance from their God.

"Then came David. He was a man after God's own heart. Yes, he sinned. In fact, he sinned horrifically. But we know from the Psalms he wrote that he was repentant with a repentance that God understood. He was promised a son who would reign forever.

"Solomon, King David's son, built the temple and the glory of the Lord filled it. This was wonderful, but Solomon's downfall was the worshiping of foreign idols. My Father drew so close, yet was pushed away by Solomon's sin.

"Not long after this, of course, the nation was divided into two kingdoms. Why? Sin. Sin brought exile and loss of the temple. It was a terrible time for my people.

"My Father is known for two paradoxical characteristics: his righteousness and his love. My Father's righteousness demands that sin be punished. Yet he wishes to redeem his people because of his love.

"The people of Israel and Judah were punished, but they deserved more than they received. Though they deserved death, destruction, and annihilation, they received exile, the hope of repatriation, and the coming of the Messiah who would make all things right."

'Isa motions with his hand for Jesus to stop and take a breath. "So, what you're saying is that Allah's love won out over his righteousness?"

Jesus smiles and says, "Absolutely. It's as if my Father put his righteousness on hold—or at least the necessity of seeing his righteousness vindicated quickly. His love pushed him to seek their redemption.

"The prophet Jeremiah wrote about the new covenant and new heart that would be given to the people of my Father.[13] The Almighty would actually draw close to his people by—now don't take this wrong—by getting inside them! He promised a new heart, a new law, and his Spirit.[14] He promised, guaranteed his covenant would be effective. How? God would do it himself! In a single day God would remove the sin of his people. His love would triumph![15]

"When the time was right, my Father did exactly what he had promised. The promised Messiah came and on a single day removed the guilt, shame, and fear associated with the sin of all humanity. The anger of my Father—his righteousness, if you will—was overcome by the love he has for all people.

"And soon, very soon, the Messiah will go back to the Father and leave the Holy Spirit to live *with* his people and *inside* his people, thus fulfilling exactly what he said he would do.

"I think this is one of the major differences between you and me, 'Isa. You are in the line of the prophets who have come again and again with the same message. I, on the other hand, come in the line of the prophets, not to repeat their message but to fulfill it."

Jesus looks closely at `Isa and asks, "So, what do you think?"

`Isa draws a long breath and says, "You know, that's some story. And that is exactly our problem. We Jews are too full of ourselves. Everything revolves around us. What has Allah done for us? What is he going to do next? The Jews have overestimated the purpose, intent, and ministry of Messiah. The Holy Qur'an gives the right explanation of Messiah's role."

"And what is that?" asks Jesus with a quizzical look on his face.

"I know you won't like this, but here it is. First, the idea of Messiah is divinely inspired by Allah (most glorious is He). Unfortunately, this revelation has been tampered with. We Jews wanted a redeemer so bad we created one. We so much longed for the restoration of Israel that we are still waiting for Messiah to come. The fact that Messiah who came did not fit the preconceived notion of Messiah is part of the problem.

"Second, the Holy Qur'an tells us who Messiah is and what he does. Messiah is strictly a Jewish prophet. He is not a king or priest or some type of universal savior. That is part of the corruption we Jews brought to our own Scriptures.

"Third, since we Jews have been waiting so long for Messiah, a further development of the term has taken place, that he will be the one who ushers in some kind of millennial kingdom in which everything that is wrong will be put right. In other words, he will come and establish a kingdom. But this is not Messiah of the Holy Qur'an at all.

"As I said earlier," `Isa says, shrugging his shoulders, "you're too dramatic! You've always got a story. But why all the suffering and melodrama? Our Lord is so great and powerful that he can forgive whenever he wants, however he wants, and whomever he wants."

Jesus replies, "Which makes me wonder how a believer knows or understands that he or she is forgiven? Is it merely confession that brings forgiveness? Is it sacrifice? Is it doing a certain amount of good deeds? How can people know they are forgiven?"

"No one knows," `Isa says, "until the final day."

Jesus says, "Let me tell you a story. Once there was a paralyzed man brought to me.[16] I sensed there was hope for healing, that those who brought him had faith. I looked down at the man, as he was lying on a portable bed, and I said, 'Take courage, son. Your sins are forgiven.'"

Jesus is laughing now. "Well, that didn't go over very well with some of my critics! I knew they were thinking, 'Blasphemy!' I also knew this could lead to some serious charges before the Sanhedrin.

"Then I said, 'Why are you thinking evil thoughts? What's easier to say: "Your sins are forgiven"'—which would mean they wouldn't see any outward change because it's not like we change color when we are forgiven—'or is it easier to say, "Get up and walk?"' Of course, that would be more difficult, because it would be a visible miracle. Ironically, it's the same power of God that heals and forgives. All this sent my critics reeling when I told the paralyzed man to get up and walk away."

`Isa says, "Yes, I also healed the lame."

"But my point," Jesus says, "is that the man knew he was forgiven because he was healed. His healing was evidence that I, the Son of Man, the Messiah, have authority to forgive sins. The healing of his body was an illustration of the wholeness brought to him by the presence of the kingdom of God."

`Isa again nods his head knowingly. "I'm aware of your claim to forgive, but it's only by the permission of Allah. However, it's not until the last hour that we will discover if forgiveness has been ultimately granted."

Jesus chuckles. "`Isa, that means that the drama of which you accuse me is simply delayed to the final act of the Islamic play. Whereas my followers know right away in Act One that forgiveness of sin is granted through belief, Muslims must wait it out to the finale to discover if they like the ending!"

`Isa counters, "No, there is no drama for the true followers of our Lord. Your illustration of a drama doesn't fit Islam. Your drama assumes certain things that cannot be accurate of our Lord's true religion."[17]

Jesus asks, "Such as?"

"Well, for one thing," he begins, "you make forgiveness a narrowly focused act that takes place once and for all. The forgiveness of *al-Khaliim*, *al-Sabuur*[18] (glorious and exalted is He) is continuous. It is not confined to one place, at one time, by one man. It is the good pleasure of our Lord to forgive and forgive and forgive again."[19]

Jesus says, "I disagree with your understanding of my assumption, but let me ask you this: What are the conditions, if any, that must be met in order to have forgiveness?"

'Isa is slowing his pace with this question, and he finally comes to a stop. Jesus stops and partially turns to him as well.

Looking at Jesus and placing both hands over his face with a downward motion, he says, "Praise Allah! A very good question and one that will give all praise and glory to our Lord as you hear about him!"

As 'Isa speaks, his hands are moving with emphasis. "I have already mentioned that Allah (glorious and exalted is He) is forgiving and most merciful. If anyone does wrong and then seeks the forgiveness of Allah, that person will find that Allah is forgiving and merciful.[20]

"You see, Jesus, all we have to do is ask! Ask for forgiveness and it is given to you. Now how is that any different from your offering forgiveness to the lame man?"

Jesus is standing with his hands on his chest, his right hand pulling on a loose thread dangling from his cuff. "I suppose . . ." He pauses and then continues, "I suppose the main difference is that the lame man *was* forgiven, as evidenced by his healing, a healing performed by the Son of Man because he has the authority to forgive sin. Do you, 'Isa, have authority to forgive sin?"

A shudder comes over 'Isa and he exclaims, "I ask forgiveness of Allah! No. Such authority is only in the purview of the Lord (glorious and exalted is He). And Jesus, you still haven't answered my question! You offered forgiveness to the lame man, but what did he do to merit it? Did he ask for forgiveness? Did he repent? Did he mend his ways? No! None of that took place. You did exactly what you say God does. Do you go around forgiving wherever, and whomever, and whenever you feel like it?"

'Isa looks as if he has caught Jesus unawares.

Solemnly, Jesus says, "The cedar tree only gives birth to the cedar. In other words, from the forgiver, forgiveness comes."

Jesus then quickly follows up his proverb with a story. "There was once a father with two sons.[21] One day the younger son said to the father, 'Give me my inheritance' (the son was all but wishing his father was dead). The father did as he requested and watched his son leave the family for the land of the Gentiles. What did the boy do with his money? He squandered it on wine, women, and song. When his money was spent, he was left with no friends, no job, no food. Things were so bad for the son that he took the job of feeding swine and even resorted to eating their food!

"One day the son came to his senses. 'What am I doing here? I'm going to leave here, return to my father and say, "Father, I've sinned before heaven and against you. I'm not worthy to be your son, so I offer myself to you as your slave."' And that's what he did. He began the long journey home.

"The father had been waiting all this time for the return of his son. And on that day when the son did return, the father saw him while he was still a long way off. The old man hiked up his tunic—showing those knobby knees and skinny legs to his own disgrace—and ran to his son. He threw his arms around the son with the embrace of forgiveness. The son never even had a chance to ask for forgiveness. The father accepted him back as his son and restored his rightful place in the family, bringing harmony and balance between father and son again.

"Unfortunately, the older brother who had stayed loyal and faithful to his father did not embrace his wayward brother. He was, in fact, angry at the father and the brother. He felt slighted in spite of the fact that the family was once again whole."

Jesus pauses briefly here. The pace of his story has been measured, thoughtful, deliberate.

With a bit quicker pace, Jesus says, "'Isa, I've told that story a thousand times, I guess. It's a wonderful picture of who the heavenly Father is and how he treats all of his wayward children. Have you figured out why the father did not allow the son to ask for forgiveness to show his repentance?"

`Isa says, "Yes, it's simple, really. The father has the power to do so. He could've demanded his son's repentance, but chose not to."

"Hmmm. I'm not sure I'd agree with your assessment. I think it's better to see the father embracing the son with forgiveness, knowing that the shame of the sin is now on the father. That is, the father disgraces himself—remember the lifting of the tunic and running towards his son, all rather disgraceful actions for an old man in our culture, wouldn't you agree?—in order to bring benefit to the sinful son. It's not that the father by the wave of his hand dismisses the sin as if it never existed. No, the father embraced the pain, the shame, and the disgrace of the son in order to forgive him. The father bore the punishment, which in this case was shame and dishonor. The father took all of that on himself. The son was set free from the shame of sin because the father bore the shame. The sin was forgiven as the father bore the dishonor.

"I respectfully suggest that when Allah offers forgiveness it is often as if the sin never existed. There is no consequence to be ameliorated, right?"

`Isa is thinking, so Jesus says, "But my Father does not treat sin in this manner. Sin is an action that requires punishment, propitiation, satisfaction, justice. When the old man takes on the shame of his son, he actually bears the punishment of that sin. The shamefulness of the son's actions is placed on the father, who willingly takes the burden."

Jesus continues, "Isn't it true that in order to gain forgiveness a person must follow Muhammad as prophet,[22] convert to Islam,[23] or give up *shirk*?[24] A thief must repent and amend for his sin.[25] But what about the glutton or the lazy . . . or the slothful? What does your Holy Book say about those? Still others must repent, believe, and do works of righteousness.[26] And does a person gain forgiveness by simply asking for it,[27] or by doing a good deed?[28]

"`Isa, you know that each of these are categories for obtaining forgiveness, but in the end all that we really know about obtaining forgiveness from Allah is that it's given whenever, and to whomever, and however he decides. Forgiveness is given without taking into consideration the cost of the sin or the notion of sinfulness."

`Isa is slightly shaking his head. "Jesus, there is a simple explanation for each of these categories. They refer to specific situations. They are not meant for every person at all times."

Jesus asks, "And what is the context for each of those occasions?"

"You know as well as I do," `Isa says, "that the context of verses in the Holy Qur'an is virtually impossible to know. We have to rely on the traditions of the Prophet to give us the context of any given verse."

Jesus answers, "Yes, I know—that's why I asked." He pauses a second and says, "But let's not beat a dead horse."

Both turn from each other as if on signal and begin walking again. They walk a few minutes in silence, the shuffling of feet the only sound they share. Then Jesus begins the conversation again.

"You said something earlier that struck me, and I'm sure you'll agree with me. I kind of leaped to the conclusion that someone replaced you on the cross. But this wouldn't make sense in light of the Almighty's character, would it? This would make him a trickster or a schemer. Why, it would even make the Almighty a liar.[29] I'm sure you'd agree."

`Isa says, "Absolutely. My Lord is the best of planners. He is not one who practices magic tricks. He knows everything and is perfect in all his ways. Allah (glorious and exalted is He) did not replace me on the cross. The Word of Allah nowhere states that there was a replacement for me. That it was made to appear to them that I was on the cross merely refers to the alleged crucifixion. The Jews only thought they had killed me. Obviously," `Isa stops, putting his hands on his chest, and says triumphantly, "they didn't. Here I am!"

Taking just a few more steps, Jesus comes to a stop and turns toward `Isa. His tone rises half an octave. "Wait, I don't get it. The Jews didn't kill you, but were only convinced they did. And it was your Lord who made them think so. So he is the best of tricksters! And what is accomplished by allowing you to live rather than dying?"

`Isa's brow furls. He squints. The sun's angle catches him in the eyes. He says, "My death would have accomplished nothing. In fact, all it would've done is to discredit our Lord. After all, I'm Messiah."

Jesus objects, "But certainly other prophets were killed.[30] Were their deaths without value? Did they die in vain?"

`Isa answers, "Yes, other prophets were killed, but I was spared."

Jesus begins, "So, to make a distinction between prophets . . ."[31]

`Isa finishes Jesus' sentence. "So, to make a distinction between the prophets (may he be pleased with them all) is to commit sin. Allah (glorious and exalted is He) has commanded his servants not to create differences between his apostles. All the messengers of Allah were of the same mind, having the same mission and the same message.

"But most certainly, nothing constrains Allah! Nothing keeps him from making exceptions among the prophets. The most highly honored apostle is Muhammad (peace be upon him), because he is the final prophet, given the final book with the message for all humanity. Among all the prophets, he is the only universal prophet. But I am second among the highly honored prophets. I am Messiah. I had a special birth. I have special titles not shared by other apostles. It is my mother who is the only woman in Scripture to be highly honored. And I had many miracles to authenticate my message.

"So, if the Lord (glorious and exalted is He) chooses to exalt one or two of his messengers over the others, is it right? He can't do anything that is less than good and righteous. But his servants are not to make the distinction of one over another."

The two have begun walking again. Jesus is about to answer when the road, which has been in a slow curve to the north, finally straightens out, providing the travelers a new vista. The day is clear, the hills to the north and south of them are distinct, and so is the city before them: Jerusalem. This is their first hint that they are very close to their destination. They stop to savor the moment.

The temple stands out in the walled city. The temple's whiteness contrasts sharply with the dull brown of the city walls, the red tiled roofs of many surrounding buildings, and the green of the nearby hills and valleys.

With the renewed exhilaration the sight provides, they walk with a fairly rapid and steady gait. It looks like Jerusalem is perhaps a bit less than an hour away.

A Grievous Penalty

Al-Maeda 5:73

They do blaspheme who say: God is one of three in a Trinity: for there is no god except One Allah. If they desist not from their word (of blasphemy) verily a grievous penalty will befall the blasphemers among them.

Deuteronomy 6:4

Hear, O Israel! The LORD our God, the LORD is one!

A s the two draw closer to Jerusalem, ironically a pig passes by, loose from its pen. There is no swineherd chasing after it. It seems to think it owns the road. The little squealer probably belongs to someone raising them for the Roman soldiers garrisoned in Jerusalem. It's not all that unusual to see pigs in Israel.

`Isa looks down at the pig and says, "Pass in peace."

"Why did you say that to the pig?" Jesus asks.

`Isa replies, "I hate to accustom my tongue to evil.[1] Remember that dog that we saw earlier?" Jesus nods.

"His teeth are white," `Isa retorts, "but his stench is foul!"[2]

"Well said, `Isa. 'He who conceals hatred has lying lips, and he who spreads slander is a fool.'"[3]

`Isa says, "I'm glad we agree. We most assuredly have our differences. It seems that as we've talked, we've mostly agreed to disagree."

"True," Jesus replies.

`Isa states, "And our differences seem to have come about because of our followers. For instance, I think it must be your followers who make you what you claim to be: the Son of God. The Holy Qur'an is very clear: Allah (glorious and exalted is He) doesn't take to himself a son[4] nor does he beget a son.[5]

"I mean," `Isa continues, pointing toward the sky, "don't you agree that our Lord is one and eternal, that he does not beget, nor is he begotten, and that there is no one like him?"[6]

Jesus answers, "Absolutely. Hear, O Israel, the Lord your God is one.[7] And the Creator certainly doesn't beget in the same manner as humans. And most assuredly, he has not been begotten himself. He is eternal."

`Isa crinkles his brow in mock surprise. "That's wonderful to hear! For all our differences, it's good to agree on such a major premise. So, you fully and clearly renounce being the Son of God? I certainly renounce it for myself."[8]

Jesus stops. `Isa stops, too, a wondering look on his face. He begins walking again, and Jesus catches up.

Turning to Jesus, `Isa asks, "What? What did I say?"

Jesus answers, "It's all right. I was just thinking. It's true. The title Son of God can be troubling. Although imagine if I were to say that because I was raised in Nazareth I am a son of Nazareth. Would that cause problems? Or if I said I'm a son of the road,[9] is that a problem?"

`Isa has clearly been waiting for this question. There is enthusiasm in his voice. "To say I am the Son of God is to make our Lord do something vulgar with my mother."

A surprised Jesus says, "Vulgar? How is the overshadowing of God's Spirit on my mother vulgar? She was found to be with child by the Spirit of the Holy One.[10] I was conceived by the Spirit[11] when he overshadowed my mother.[12] What in any of this is vulgar?"

`Isa is just as surprised. "Wait, do you, right here and now, deny ever saying, 'Worship me and my mother as gods in derogation of Allah?'"[13]

Jesus states calmly, "Isn't it interesting that your Holy Book accuses me of something I never did and something I never taught?"

"It's more than interesting," `Isa interjects. "It's what your followers have said about you. It's what your disciples believe."

Jesus takes a deep breath and says, "`Isa, give me a second here to develop this thought.

"According to your book, my disciples believe my mother and I, along with my Father, are gods. And as a result of the union of Mary and my Father, the Trinity was born when I, the Son of God, was born.

"According to your book, all these things are true, but according to my own statements and the statements of the prophets and those through whom revelation came by inspiration, none of this is true.

"So, here's my question: What beliefs is your book explaining and condemning if they are from neither the Torah nor the Gospels?"

It's `Isa's turn to stop now. Jesus slows down and stops with him. `Isa looks genuinely confused. "Wait. Do you completely deny that you or your followers believe any of these statements in the Holy Qur'an?"

Jesus nods and replies, "It is as you have said."

There is a pause, and then a rapid-fire response: "All right, perhaps your disciples do not believe such a thing, but those who follow me, Messiah, certainly do."

"Then think of the implications," Jesus says. "The statements attributed to me and my followers are patently false. Yet your book insists my followers believe I said to worship me and my mother as gods. This incorrect evaluation implicates you, not me."

Up to this point Jesus has been nonchalant in his tone, but he now begins to speak with greater intensity, almost as if he is willing 'Isa to catch what he is saying.

"What I mean is this. Those who believe I would say such a thing are not my followers, and yet, they are called followers of Messiah, right?"

'Isa mutters, "Hmm."

Jesus continues, "So, if they are not my followers, but are followers of another messiah, they must be *your* followers."

'Isa's eyes brighten with comprehension. "Ahh. So, you're suggesting it's possible these things really *are* believed, but that they are incorrectly understood by my disciples. Yes, I see your point. My followers believe I said such a thing, and in fact, while I never did, it is truly my followers who are mistaken."

Jesus smiles. "Yes. Your followers, not mine, say and believe these things because you are the Messiah of Islam and I am not. It's really plain, don't you think?

"So, we are agreed, then?" Jesus asks. "We are not the same Messiah. You are al-Masih of the Holy Qur'an. I'm ha-mashiach of the Holy Scriptures."

The two men start walking again. Both are deeply involved with their own thoughts, barely looking at the surrounding countryside.

Then Jesus asks, "What conclusion would you draw if you heard your followers described as ill-bred, unwashed, uneducated camel lovers?"

'Isa says, "I would know that whoever said such a thing had never met me or my followers. In fact, I would assume that what they said about me and my followers was probably true about them."

Jesus laughs heartily and says, "I couldn't agree more! Such a remark shows a real ignorance of who your followers are.

"The same is true—and I say this with all respect—the same thing is true of your book if what it says about me and my followers is not true! Whoever penned the words 'Worship me and my mother as gods in derogation of Allah' never met me or my followers."

'Isa says, "Now wait a minute. That's not true, because you have disciples during the time of Prophet Muhammad (peace and blessings be upon him). As a matter of fact, his uncle, Waraqa, is a one of your follow-ers.[14] Furthermore, the Prophet of our Lord sends his people to Abyssinia where they receive refuge from the king, who is also one of your disciples. Why, there are even disciples of yours who become believers by hearing the preaching of Muhammad (peace and blessings upon him).[15] Surely you don't deny this?"

Jesus answers, "No, I don't deny it. However, what I deny is that my followers are those described in your book. The book confuses them with the followers of another Jesus."

`Isa gasps, "A different Jesus? What do you mean? There are others . . . others like you?"

"There will come people," Jesus begins, "who will declare things about me that are not true, yet they will call themselves my followers.

"For instance, there will come a time when some will believe the Messiah is the same as the Father and that because the Messiah suffered, the Father also suffered.[16] Another teaching will come about that my mother, Mary, is *theotokos*,[17] and it seems this influences the view of those who will follow Muhammad. Do you see what I'm saying, `Isa?"

`Isa muses and adds, "Perhaps . . . perhaps, but ultimately it's all the same religion. When Allah (glorious and exalted is He) speaks, it is true. How can the words of our Lord be wrong? They can't, so I think that what we have is the Qur'an speaking to the believers it encounters. It doesn't matter which Jesus they follow. What it says about their beliefs is accurate, authoritative, and corrective."

"Yes, I agree," Jesus nods his head. "So, I guess it's possible to say that the Qur'an really doesn't speak about me, the Messiah whose life and ministry is found in the Holy Scriptures. Rather, it speaks about the Messiah of the third, fourth, fifth and sixth centuries. I become a Messiah who is incorrectly understood by people who will call themselves my disciples at that time."

There is a low hedge running parallel to the road. `Isa is running his hand over the top of it. He snags a leaf and inspects it and then says, "All right, I understand what the Trinity is not. It is not Allah, you, and your mother. So what is it?"

Jesus motions for the two of them to sit down under a nearby tree. Its branches are bountiful with leaves, perfect for shade. The two sit under the tree, neither leaning against it. The ground under the tree is barren of grass, but neither seems to care.

Jesus says, "Before I tell you a story, let me ask a question. Are there any other verses in your book about the way the People of the Book view the Almighty?"

`Isa begins an Arabic chant:

> "They do blaspheme who say:
> Allah is one of three in a Trinity:
> for there is no god except One Allah.
> If they desist not from their word (of blasphemy) verily
> a grievous penalty will befall the blasphemers among
> them."[18]

"And how do you understand the verse?" Jesus asks.

"The People of the Book believe the Magnificent One is three: the Father, as you call him, is just one of the three gods called Trinity. It is a blasphemous and perniciously evil doctrine. It will be most severely punished by our Lord at the last hour. Our Lord is one. He is *not* three."

Jesus says, "I agree that the Creator is not three, but one. Rather than give you definitions, let me tell you a story.

"The Lord God made the heavens and the earth and all the animals, and on the earth he created a beautiful garden. And in that garden he put the first man and woman. They were to tend the garden, and care for it as if it were their own. And the man and the woman were given one commandment: 'You are free to eat from any tree in the garden; but you must not eat from the tree of the knowledge of good and evil, for when you eat of it you will surely die.'

"Now also in the garden was an animal more crafty than any of the wild animals the Lord God had made. He would come to the woman and whisper, 'Did God really say, You must not eat from any tree in the garden?'"

Not able to restrain himself, `Isa adds, "Satan makes them promises and creates in them false desires, but Satan's promises are nothing but deception."[19]

Jesus nods his head and, continuing, says, "The woman replied, 'We are allowed to eat from all the trees but one. It is in the middle of the garden. We must not touch it for it brings death.'

"'You will not surely die,' the serpent said to the woman. 'For God knows that when you eat of it your eyes will be opened, and you will be like God, knowing good and evil.'

"The woman saw that the fruit of the forbidden tree was quite beautiful. She saw it was perfect for eating and for attaining the wisdom being denied her. 'That's not fair,' she thought. So she took the fruit and she ate it. She gave it to her husband, who was there the whole time, and he ate it."

`Isa is fully engrossed with the story.

Jesus asks, "What happened? Did they die right there?" He pauses.

"No," `Isa responds.

"Right," Jesus says, "but the process of death had begun, like a branch separated from its life-giving trunk. They looked fine, but were in fact dead.

"They broke the Lord God's commandment. They felt guilt. They violated their relationship with the Lord God, and felt shame for having dishonored their Lord. They lost their rightful position. They were afraid. They were most certainly frightened by the Lord God, and not without good reason!"

At this point, Jesus folds his arms across his chest. He says, "The Lord God was in the garden when the man heard him coming."

Jesus looks directly at `Isa. He repeats the statement quite deliberately, emphasizing *in* and *coming* the second time: "The Lord God was *in* the garden when the man heard him *coming*."

`Isa responds, "Actually, Allah (glorious and exalted is He) said, 'Did I not forbid you that tree and tell you that Satan was an avowed enemy unto you?[20] But . . . he was not *in* the garden."

"All right," Jesus says, "but yours is an argument from silence, not Scripture. On the other hand, Moses' account specifically says God was in the garden."

`Isa, a shade of indignation coloring his face, looks up at Jesus and says, "It is impossible that the Lord would be physically present in the garden. This is to demean our Lord, for he is eternal and majestic, unlike his creation in any way! No, your story makes no sense. You are suggesting something our Lord would never do."

Jesus ponders this for a few seconds. "`Isa, could the Creator of the universe do what the story I've told you suggests? In other words, is it within the power and scope of the Almighty to walk in the garden with his creation, or is it something that he is unable to do?"

With no hesitation, `Isa says, "Yes, our Lord could, if he chose, walk in the garden. He could take on human form. But he has not chosen to do so."

Jesus doesn't let this statement gain any momentum. "So, if the Creator could . . . just for argument's sake, he might take on human form. What would happen to the universe if he did such a thing? Would it collapse into a vacuum because the Almighty was not in his rightful place? Or it is possible the world would continue to function, because he is, after all, the Creator and sustainer of the universe?"

`Isa seems not to have considered the latter option. He is about to speak when Jesus breaks into his thoughts: "The Holy Scriptures reveal to us a Creator who is able to be in the garden at the same time as he fills the universe with his presence to the same degree and measure as if he were not in the garden. The evidence of his ability to do such a marvelous feat is that the universe did not, in fact, disappear, shimmer, shake, or quiver into extinction.

"The Creator is so powerful and mighty that he is able to be everywhere and, at the very same time, manifest himself in a garden with two of his creatures.

"`Isa, the God of the universe is not limited by our imaginations or by the silence of a book."

`Isa is slowly shaking his head from disbelief that Jesus could believe such things. He says, "You may choose to believe this about our Lord, but I know he would never stoop so low as to limit himself to this world. There is no need. There is no drama that demands such an act."

Jesus simply shrugs and says, "Well, this is how we should understand the Creator. Your book uses the word *Trinity*, but then it doesn't describe God as the Holy Scriptures do. I'm just trying to help you see there's more to this Trinity idea than what's in your own book."

`Isa says, "The book of your followers speaks about the Father, the Son, and the Holy Spirit. I count three. One plus one plus one is three. You can't escape that, Jesus."

"Who says I'm trying to escape it?" Jesus asks. "All I'm hoping to do is get you to think differently about the Creator."

Almost indignant, `Isa replies, "I don't need to think differently about our Lord! All I need to know about him is in the Holy Book. And you still haven't convinced me about the truth of the Trinity."

Shrugging, Jesus says, "Nor am I trying to. Doesn't it seem a bit strange to you that we're talking about a view of the Creator that we both agree is not explicitly mentioned in the Holy Scriptures, but *is* referred to in your book—and wrongly at that? And yet your book claims to have existed from eternity past."

`Isa is considering these words and then says, "This only proves the divinity of the Qur'an, doesn't it? It's a book that not only speaks of the past with accuracy, but it can reveal the future as well."

Jesus says, "I think we've wandered a bit from my helping you appreciate who the Creator is according to the Scriptures. So, let me tell you another story."

`Isa nods his head. "I'm listening."

"Moses," Jesus begins, "was in the desert with his flock, wandering with them through the wilderness as they grazed throughout the day. When he and his flock came close to Mount Horeb, he saw a burning bush, but it wasn't being consumed by the fire."[21]

`Isa nods his head, "Yes, I know this story well. Prophet Moses (peace and blessings be upon him) went to the bush, hoping to bring back a coal to begin his own fire or perhaps to meet someone there."[22]

Jesus asks, "And what did he see when he got closer to the bush?"

"Well," `Isa answers, "he heard the voice of the Lord: 'O Moses, verily I am your Lord. Therefore, put off your shoes; thou art in the sacred valley Tuwa. I have chosen thee; listen then to the inspiration.'"

"Oh," Jesus says, "didn't Moses also hear, 'Blessed are those in the Fire and those around: and Glory to Allah the Lord of the Worlds! O Moses! verily I am Allah the Exalted in Might the Wise!'?"[23]

Jesus pauses, then adds, "Or was it that he heard, 'O Moses! verily I am Allah the Lord of the Worlds!'?"[24]

`Isa grins. "Jesus, he heard all of that."

Jesus returns the grin and says, "Good. Moses heard the voice of the Lord. I agree. But doesn't that trouble you?"

`Isa replies, "No. The statement is very clear. The voice of our Lord speaks with Prophet Moses. But if you're trying to make the point that God has a voice and therefore has lungs, throat, tongue, teeth, and a mouth just like a human, this is *not* how our Lord is to be understood."

"No, that's not my point at all," Jesus responds. "In fact, I completely agree with you. But the fact that Moses heard God's voice at a specific time and place—that Moses' ears picked up the sound—none of this bothers you? Wait . . . you don't think this was a vision or dream, do you?"

"No," `Isa draws his breath, "but I do think you're assuming too much. You're assuming Moses literally heard the voice of God."

Jesus answers, "I don't assume anything that those who will read the story don't assume! Anyway, regardless how the Almighty did this—with a voice unlike anything human in origin or by some miraculous means—the point remains: Moses heard the voice of God. Just as the Creator entered the garden and spoke with Adam and Eve, he did the same with Moses. The Creator is located in a physical place."

"No, I can't agree," `Isa objects. "You're making more from the story than is actually there. Our Lord is not man, nor is he a voice, nor is he a bush!"

Jesus says, "I'm only trying to share with you how God reveals himself to humanity. If even this can't be understood, how can such a belief as the Trinity ever be understood?"

`Isa laughs, "Jesus, that's the most intelligent thing you've said all day!"

Jesus smiles. "But wait, there's a bit more to the story I began earlier."

"You mean about Prophet Moses?" `Isa asks.

"No," Jesus answers. "About our first parents in the garden. It seems the man and woman were hiding in the nearby trees after their act of disobedience. The very trees from which the Lord God said they could eat were now hiding them, separating them from the Lord God.

"The Lord God called to them, 'Where are you?' Of course, the Lord God knew where they were, but don't you think it's an interesting question, `Isa?"

"I suppose so," he says and then he adds, "It's certainly not part of the story as I know it."

Jesus says, "And the Lord God then began a series of questions to the quivering, fearful, shamed, and guilty couple: 'Who told you that you were naked? Have you eaten from the tree that I commanded you not to eat from? What is this you have done?'

"When confronted with his sin, the man blamed the woman. And when she was confronted with her sin, the woman blamed the serpent. As I mentioned earlier, sin cannot go unpunished, so the Lord God pronounced a curse on the serpent:

> Because you have done this, cursed are you above all the livestock and all the wild animals! You will crawl on your belly and you will eat dust all the days of your life. And I will put enmity between you and the woman, and between your offspring and hers; he will crush your head, and you will strike his heel.[25]

To this `Isa adds, "And from that day until this, Satan is the one who seduces us, assaults us, ambushes us!"[26]

Jesus nods in agreement. "Indeed, Satan is the Father of Lies. He is the Evil One. `Isa, did you hear the threat to Satan about his problems with the offspring of the woman?"

`Isa says, "Yes, you said that between the offspring of the woman and of the serpent there would be enmity."

"And what would happen between them?"

"The offspring of the serpent," `Isa recalls, "bites his heel. The offspring of the woman crushes his head." And then he adds, "None of this is in the story as I know it. How do you understand it? Sounds like another one of your proverbs."

Jesus states, "I'll get to the explanation in just a minute.

"But next, the Lord God punished the woman. She will have increased pain in childbirth and she will desire her husband, though he'll rule over her.

"And then the Lord God punished the evil deed of the man with the promise that his work of finding food would not be easy. The sin of the man brought about a curse to the very soil his livelihood depended on. Finally, just as the Lord God had promised, he told the man that since he had been created from the dust of the earth, so he would return. That is, he would die."

Again, Jesus pauses. He looks like a master storyteller enjoying his craft.

With a wave of his hand, Jesus says, "Now, that's still not the end of the story. The man and woman were banished from the garden. A cherubim and a flaming sword that swung back and forth kept them out.

"But before they were banished, the Lord God did something very surprising."

Jesus is looking directly at `Isa.

"Yes?" `Isa asks. "What did he do?"

Jesus does not immediately answer. Then, after brushing his hair out of his eyes, he begins, "The man and woman clothed themselves with fig leaves. Interesting, huh? The trees—first they can't eat from one of them, then our father and mother hide behind them, and now they take the leaves for clothes. Well, the Lord God saw this, and he knew it was an inadequate attempt to cover themselves. Do you know what he did?"

`Isa answers in what might be taken as a faintly mocking tone, "I don't know. Did he clothe them himself?"

Jesus smiles, "That's right! He saw their pitiful attempt at covering their shame and did something about it. He gave them the skin of an animal as new clothing.

"`Isa, he gave them the skin of an innocent animal, an animal that had to die in order for this to take place, right?"

"Unless," `Isa says, "our Lord simply created the skin for this purpose."

Jesus says, "Yes, I suppose that's possible, but it doesn't seem likely considering what happens next."

`Isa asks, "All right, what happens next?"

"Remember the offspring of the serpent and of the woman?" Jesus asks.

`Isa nods his head.

"I'm going to connect it to the death of an innocent victim to cover the man and woman."

`Isa grunts, "Huh?"

Jesus says, "Let's go sit under that tree. It's hot."

The two make their way to a large broad-leafed tree off the road in front of them and to the right. They stand under it, and Jesus starts up again, "After the man and woman were banished from the garden, the Scriptures give us story after story of how the Lord God called out a man, say like Abraham, or a woman like Rahab the harlot, or a tribe like Levi, and then he even calls a nation, Israel, to be his chosen people. His purpose in doing so was to show all the nations of the earth how a particular people—the people of Abraham—are in a covenant relationship with the Lord God.

"The Lord God calls his people to be a light to the nations,[27] to be the means by which the Lord God's salvation reaches the ends of the earth,[28] to be the people that attract the nations to the beauty of their Lord and God.[29]

"But after many years, the people of the Lord God neglected their role to the nations. The honor of being called his people became an end in itself. In fact, they began to think that the only way to serve, honor, and worship the Lord God was the way they themselves did it. So the temple took on greater significance. If a person wanted to worship the Lord God, it had to be done in the temple. And they began trying to protect the Torah with suffocating traditions. My people paid greater attention to these human laws than to the words of God. The idea of Israel as the people of God had become more a birthright of privilege and prestige than a blessing to the nations."

Jesus pauses and then says, "In the fullness of time[30] the deliverer, the Messiah, was sent to complete the task that Israel had neglected for so many years. Whereas Israel had focused worship on the temple, I showed them that worship is done in spirit and truth, not in a certain location.[31] Whereas Israel had suffocated and strangled the Lord God's words with oral traditions, I fulfilled the law of Moses.[32] And although Israel had been habitually attempting to reestablish the kingdom of David through force, I came as a suffering servant."[33]

`Isa is silently mulling over all of this.

Jesus asks, "So how did I accomplish all this? What did I do to fulfill all God's purposes in the temple, the Torah, and Israel?"

`Isa looks at Jesus. He shrugs. It seems he really doesn't know.

Jesus says, "This is the work of Messiah, `Isa. When I was nailed to the cross, I took on myself the sin of the world. I became that innocent victim that covered the shame of those who have sinned. I, the Messiah of the Lord God, came in order to die on the cross, in order to restore the honor, the innocence, and the power of the individual in a covenant relationship to the Creator. I, the Messiah of the Lord God, came in order to do for Israel what it could not do for itself. And so the animal skin that covered Adam and Eve is really a picture of what I have accomplished by dying on the cross and standing before you here today."

'Isa is ready to move on. He makes a start for the road, then stops and says, "Jesus, that's a very interesting story." He hesitates, clears his throat, and says, "I would believe it if it were in the Holy Book."

Jesus returns his look. "Yes, it's an interesting story. It explains just about everything about the Lord of the Universe. Too bad it's not in your Holy Book, because there are many good things there."

Their pace is leisurely. It's almost as if they are both willing their journey to take longer than it should.

Jesus asks, "If I may, there is another way to discuss the Lord of the Universe. You may not have fully appreciated my story, and I can understand that. So, let me ask some questions and we can see where that takes us."

"That's fine," 'Isa replies.

"Good, then let's talk about God's oneness. You brought up the word some time ago and I really didn't pursue it. I'd like to now. When you said I 'breached God's oneness,' what exactly did you mean? What is God's oneness?"

"Ahh, a most excellent question," 'Isa says. "Allah (most glorious is He) is the absolute one. He is not of several essences, but one. He is not of several personalities, but one. He is completely indivisible. Allah's oneness means he cannot have children. He is unlike anyone or anything. Nothing is like him. Allah's oneness is the most important fact about him. When we come to realize this, we know all that we need to know about him."

"Is another one of his qualities," asks Jesus, "being merciful and compassionate?"

"Yes, he is the Merciful and Compassionate. He is the Most Loving and Most Affectionate."[34]

"Good," says Jesus. "Now is Allah's oneness eternal?"

"Yes."

"Are Allah's mercy and compassion and love eternal?" Jesus asks.

"Yes, yes, and yes," 'Isa grins.

"I can understand how oneness can be eternal. It's an essential thing about Allah. But if he is one, completely indivisible, how can he be eternally merciful, compassionate, and loving?"

"That's very easy," `Isa says. "These are eternal with him because he is eternal himself."

"No, I understand that, but if mercy, compassion, and love mean anything as concepts, they require an object to which mercy, compassion, or love can be shown, right?"

`Isa thinks for a few seconds. "Yes, I see what you mean."

"Good. If Allah is eternally loving, it means he had to be *loving* something from eternity. So, let me ask, what thing has Allah been loving eternally?"

"Of course humanity has not existed for ever, so he has not been loving people eternally. The same is true of the angels and jinn, not to mention the universe. The only possible answer is that Allah is eternally loving because he tells us he is."

Jesus looks around for something to grab to help illustrate what he wants to say. "Wait here," he says.

`Isa stands on the road, arms crossed on his chest while Jesus trots off down a ravine. He disappears. There are some rustling sounds and then the cracking of a branch.

A grunt, then the sound of a branch snapping comes from the ravine. Jesus reappears, smiling victoriously and holding a gnarled branch over his head. "This branch didn't want to leave its tree," he says. "Here, you hold this." He hands it to `Isa.

Reaching out to grab the branch, the thickness of a thumb, `Isa asks, "So, what are we doing?"

"You have the branch in your hands. How long have you had it?"

`Isa says, rather skeptically, "Just a few seconds."

"That's right. So it would be wrong for me to describe you to a friend as the eternal holder of the branch, right? That is, you have not had the branch in your hand for eternity, but for a limited time. So how is that any different from saying that Allah is eternally loving when he could not love until he created something to love?"

`Isa hands the branch back to Jesus. "It's different because Allah says he is. If he says he is eternally loving, he is."

Jesus tosses the stick to the side of the road and the two begin walking again. He looks at his hand. There is no mark, welt, or bruise.

"What I am trying to get at, you see," Jesus begins, "is that Allah cannot be eternally loving or merciful or compassionate as you understand it. On the other hand, using the same terms with the same meaning, it is quite understandable—and ironically no less mysterious—that my Father and I and the Comforter can be in an eternal, loving, and compassionate relationship. The Father eternally loves the Son who eternally loves the Spirit who eternally loves the Father. If this were not true, the Father could not say, 'I am love.'"

`Isa takes all this in without showing much emotion. He somberly shakes his head and says, "Never could I say what I had no right [to say]. . . . Never said I to them aught except what Thou didst command me to say . . . 'Worship Allah, my Lord and your Lord.'"[35]

Jesus says nothing. They continue walking a bit until `Isa says, "You know, all this funny talk of yours—Allah walking in the garden, the Trinity, your misunderstanding of Allah's oneness—it can all be pinpointed on the corrupted Torah."

"`Isa, let me ask you this. Earlier we talked about the prophets knowing or not knowing the name of the Almighty. You believe it is Allah, and I believe it is 'I Am Who I Am.' I've been thinking about this question for some time, but this seems like the best time to ask. Do you think the God you serve is the same God I serve?"

`Isa muses on the question for a few seconds and then replies, "Absolutely. How could it be otherwise? There is only one Allah. All the prophets have delivered their messages for him. There is one Allah and we must worship him. This was the message of Adam, Noah, Abraham, Moses, David, and me. So, yes, while you may not know it or may disagree, there is no mistake. Allah is the God both of us serve. Let me show you that we serve the same God. Is there just one God of the universe?"

Jesus says, "Yes, of course."

"Good. Did that God create the heavens and earth in six days?"

"Yes."

"All right, did that God create Adam and Eve, placing them in the garden?"

"Yes."

"And did that God reveal himself to prophets?"

"Yes."

"And does this one God deserve all our obedience and worship?"

Jesus is nodding his head.

"So, this is how I *know* that you and I are speaking of the same God," `Isa affirms.

At this point the two hear a thudding sound coming from behind them—the sound of military boots. They turn and see a band of Roman soldiers. Coming right at the two men are about a hundred soldiers in four columns taking up the entire road.

`Isa pulls Jesus off to the side of the road to let the soldiers pass unhindered.

The centurion is easy to recognize since his is the only iron helmet with the crimson splash of a plume on the top. The soldiers are not talking as they march. Each legionnaire is equipped with the short dagger and sword that make him so formidable, the *pugio* and *gladius*. The knives are sheathed and dangle from their belts, suspended by leather straps. Each *pugio* bounces up and down in rhythm with their steps. The swords are strung from the shoulders. The shield, normally held in the left hand, is strapped to the back of each soldier to make the march easier. They pass by quickly, barely noticing two Jews on the same road.

"I am glad they didn't stop and demand we carry their cloaks," Jesus says. "That's a lot of cloaks that just went by."

"Agreed!" `Isa says.

"So, `Isa, if I see a man with a sword, is he a soldier?"

"More than likely he is."

"But if the man with the sword is using the sword to pry off the lid of an olive jar, he's probably a farmer or merchant, right?"

"All right, if you say so," `Isa says.

"Now, if a man has a sword and is killing an enemy, he's a soldier, right?"

"Yes."

"But not if the man with the sword is a zealot who is fighting a Roman soldier."

"What are you trying to say, Jesus?" `Isa asks.

"Only this: it's important to know what's important when making comparisons. Just because a man has a sword doesn't mean he's a soldier. He may as likely be a farmer, a merchant, or a rebel."

"All right, agreed, but where are you going with this?"

"Just because we agree there is a Creator," Jesus says, "that's no guarantee we are speaking of the same God. Even if we say he revealed himself to prophets, we are not necessarily speaking of the same God. What he reveals about himself is a much more important question, don't you think?"

"Perhaps," `Isa answers. "But we've been through this already. Allah has revealed himself in many books, but finally in the Holy Qur'an, a book that confirms all previous revelations.[36] The revelation of Allah in the Qur'an is the final word for humanity."

Jesus looks up and, recognizing this part of the road, says, "You know, Jerusalem is not all that far now." There's new life in their steps as the city grows near.

The Last Hour

Luqman 31:33

O mankind! do your duty to your Lord and fear (the coming of) a Day when no father can avail aught for his son nor a son avail aught for his father. Verily the promise of Allah is true: let not then this present life deceive you nor let the Chief Deceiver deceive you about Allah.

Matthew 24:30–31

At that time the sign of the Son of Man will appear in the sky, and all the nations of the earth will mourn. They will see the Son of Man coming on the clouds of the sky, with power and great glory. And he will send his angels with a loud trumpet call, and they will gather his elect from the four winds, from one end of the heavens to the other.

Isa and Jesus are encountering more people as they near the gates of Jerusalem. They appear to be mostly merchants, their camels loaded with jars of olive oil or nuts, donkeys burdened with bundles of firewood and large, bulging sacks of cloth, as well as trinkets and clanging pots and pans. The merchants are not interested in two travelers, nor do `Isa and Jesus show much interest in them.

A young boy, maybe eleven or twelve, leads his flock across the road. He is carrying a lamb, probably his pet since it does not look injured. He is in the middle of the road encouraging his flock across when Jesus yells out to him, "Shalom, young master. Is that your pet in your arms?"

The boy has a jug of water over one shoulder, a small satchel over the other. He has a staff taller than himself in one hand, the lamb in the other. The young lad looks down at the lamb. "Yes, this is Suri. She's my pet."

`Isa asks, "Where is her mother? Surely she should be able to take care of her."

"No," the boy says. He shoos on more of his flock and then says, "Her mother is dead. She died giving birth to Suri. So I'm taking care of her now."

`Isa says, "That's quite noble."

Jesus adds, "So, where are you taking your sheep now, young master?"

"Just over the next ridge there." He points toward the east, to a low hill not far away. "We'll spend the night there. I have my corral built and there's water nearby."

`Isa says, "Well, good travels to you then."

"Yes, shalom to you," Jesus adds.

The boy shoos the remaining sheep across the road and is quickly gone. His concern for the young lamb was touching.

Jesus says, "I've always had a soft spot in my heart for sheep. I was never a shepherd, but there's something about these animals that grabs my attention. I suppose it's partly because our father David was a shepherd and he wrote that beautiful psalm about the believer's relationship with the Lord God in terms of sheep, pastures, and fresh water. I've even been called the Lamb of God because I take away the sin of the world. What about you, `Isa? Are you called the Lamb of God?"

"No," he begins, "but I certainly do have a soft spot for sheep as well. And I think it's for the same reason—King David. Perhaps you know this story about him?[1]

"Once the king was in his private chambers when two men climbed over the walls and landed in the king's palace. At first, David was afraid, but the two men assured him they were only there because they need him to settle an argument.

"One man said of the other, 'This is my brother. He has ninety-nine lambs and I have just one. He is constantly after my one little ewe-lamb.'

"King David said to the man with the ninety-nine, 'You are doing wrong.'

"It was then that David realized he himself was on trial by our Lord (glorious and exalted is He). David repented of his lapse and was forgiven. From then on he enjoyed a closeness to Allah (most glorious is He)."

Jesus says, "That sounds vaguely similar to Prophet Nathan's parable to King David—yet it's not the same. So, what was David's lapse?"

"Ahh," `Isa sighs, "we don't know the sin, but it's enough for us to know that David lapsed, then repented, and Allah, *al-Khalim, al-Sabuur*, forgave him."

Jesus asks again, "You just mentioned David's final return. Did you mean that David is coming again or did you mean the Day of Judgment?"

`Isa says, "No, David does not come a second time. He found his abode in paradise as a reward for his good deeds.

"But," `Isa continues, "as for my return—"

"Wait! You come to earth a second time?" Jesus is evidently astonished.

"Oh, of course," `Isa smiles. "I return at a time known only to Allah.[2] In fact, I am one of ten signs that the final hour is upon us."[3]

"One of ten!" Jesus blurts out. "I've got to know the other nine."

"All right. In order, they are smoke, the *Dajjal*, the beast, the sun rising in the west . . ." At this, `Isa smiles. "Then there is my coming, followed by the Gog and Magog, landslides in the East, West, and Arabia, and then fire burns from Yemen."

"The Dajjal?" Jesus questions.

`Isa says, "Yes, the Dajjal is a man described by the prophet Muhammad (peace and blessings upon him), a young man who has twisted, cropped hair and one eye.[4] Muhammad said that if his followers see him they must recite this verse: 'Praise be to Allah, who hath sent to His Servant the Book, and hath allowed therein no Crookedness.'[5]

"The Dajjal shows up just outside of Medina and causes mayhem and disaster wherever he goes."

"How long does this continue?" Jesus asks.

"He will stay for forty days. One day will be as a year, one day as a month, and one day as a week, although the rest of the days will be like our own days. In other words, it will be a difficult time on the earth.

"Another thing—the way the Dajjal moves will be like a cloud driven by the wind. He will invite people to a religion other than Islam. Many will follow him because when he commands rain to fall, it falls. Crops will grow, herds will prosper, and drought will be a thing of the past.

"But not everyone he invites to his new religion will accept his invitation. There will be a group of people who reject him. The result of their rejection is his anger on them.

"When the Dajjal is challenged, the challenger is killed. But the Dajjal then resurrects the challenger."

He pauses to let that sink in, thinking Jesus needs a moment to fully grasp the situation.

`Isa continues, "Yes, the Dajjal brings his erstwhile challenger back to life. Why does he do this? The Dajjal knows the prophecies that say the Dajjal will come and kill all challengers, and in order to trick the world into thinking he is not really the Dajjal, he resurrects his challenger! But eventually this evil plan backfires.[6]

"This is when I appear for a second time. I come down in Damascus, wearing garments dyed the color of saffron.[7] I will have my hands on the wings of two angels. I will be lightly perspiring so that when I raise my head, the beads of perspiration will scatter over the earth. And when unbelievers smell the odor of my body, they will die. My breath will reach farther than anyone can see. It will be my task to hunt down and kill the Dajjal."[8]

Jesus is amazed. "I had no idea you would have such a fantastic adventure. So, after you have dispatched the Dajjal—the antichrist, I assume . . ."

'Isa nods his head at this, and Jesus asks, "What happens next?"

"The most important thing—well, at least I think it is—" 'Isa says, "is that there will be prosperity on the earth for some time. The earth will be blessed. The fruits and plants of the earth will grow large and plentiful. It will be possible for a large group of people to enjoy one pomegranate. They'll also be able to be shaded from the sun by the skin of that same pomegranate. There will be enough milk from one cow to feed hundreds of people. And the sheep—they'll do the same. In fact, a sheep's milk will feed an entire tribe.

"During the time of this wonderful blessing, Allah will send a gentle wind that will be dry and pleasing. It will even dry the perspiration from one's armpits!

"Finally, Allah will take the life of every Muslim. Only the wicked will survive, and they survive in order to face the last hour."[9]

A merchant, an old man with a sparse salt and pepper beard, is beginning to pass them on their left. The two men instinctively move to the right. The old man is leading, sometimes tugging, and often saying to his camel, who is loaded with jars of oil and trailing behind him, "Come on, you old bag of bones." The old man greets both men with a gruff "shalom" and receives their "shalom to you" in return.

It is not until the camel has passed Jesus that he asks 'Isa, "So, the last hour comes. What happens then?"

"Several things," 'Isa answers. "But first, I have to say that the prophet Muhammad (peace and blessings be upon him) will be the chief or head of all people on that day."

Jesus asks, "Chief? What do you mean by that?"

"Well, the Lord will gather all human beings in one place," `Isa begins. "The sun will be so close to everyone that all are extremely worried about being burned to cinders. It will finally dawn on them that the Day of Judgment has arrived. Recognizing their predicament, they begin asking, 'Who will intercede for us?'

"And then the suggestion is made, 'Let's go find Adam. He can intercede for us.'

"There is a tradition about that day that goes like this:

> So they will go to Adam and say to him, 'You are the father of mankind; Allah created you with His Own Hand, and breathed into you of His Spirit (meaning the spirit which he created for you); and ordered the angels to prostrate before you; so (please) intercede for us with your Lord. Don't you see in what state we are? Don't you see what condition we have reached?' Adam will say, 'Today my Lord has become angry as He has never become before, nor will ever become thereafter. He forbade me (to eat of the fruit of) the tree, but I disobeyed Him. Myself! Myself! Myself! (has more need for intercession). Go to someone else; go to Noah.'[10]

"So the people go to Noah, but when they ask Noah to intercede for them, he says he isn't able. Once he had the right, but now he doesn't. He tells them, 'Go to Abraham.' The people go to Abraham, but Abraham is unable because he told three lies. He tells them to go to Moses. But Moses tells the people he isn't able, because he killed the Egyptian. Moses sends them to me. I will not mention any sin, because I never committed any, but I'll also tell the crowd that I'm unable to intercede for them. I send them to Muhammad.

"The people come to the Prophet Muhammad (peace be upon him) and he says,

> Then I will go beneath God's Throne and fall in prostration before my Lord. And then God will guide me to such praises and glorification to Him as He has never guided anybody else before me. . . . 'O Muhammad! Raise your head. Ask,

and it will be granted. Intercede! It will be accepted.'

"So I will raise my head and say, 'My followers, O my Lord! My followers, O my Lord.'

"It will be said, 'O Muhammad! Let those of your followers who have no accounts, enter through such a gate of the gates of Paradise as lies on the right; and they will share the other gates with the people.'"[11]

"That would be something to see," says Jesus. "You've really given me something to think about."

"Yes, but my story's not over yet," Isa says. "Some of my most important acts will be, as a just ruler, to break all crosses, kill all pigs, and abolish the *jizya*."[12]

Jesus asks, "I guess it's obvious why you break the crosses and kill the pigs? Are these symbolic acts? That is, do they have meaning beyond the simple act?"

'Isa says, "Allah (glorious and exalted is He) will perfect his religion when he sends Islam to the prophet Muhammad (peace be upon him). Our Lord's chosen religion for all humanity is Islam, as I mentioned earlier. It's simple, really. No other religion is called his chosen religion, none other has been perfected, none other has been chosen by the Lord himself for his servants, and no other religion is the true religion."[13]

"So . . ." Jesus muses, his right hand scratching his chin, "you come back to earth as part of the process of finalizing the religion of Islam."

"Yes. I return to earth and all humanity faces the last hour."

Some minutes of silence pass between them. Finally, 'Isa speaks. "You know, I'm going to call all my followers together on that final day. They will be asked, 'Whom did you worship?' They will say, "Isa! We worshiped 'Isa.'

"And they will be called liars by Allah. 'God never had a wife or a son,' they are told. Then those of my followers who were obedient to our Lord (glorious and exalted is He) will remain and the others will be taken away."

Jesus remains quiet. Jesus turns to `Isa and says, "I need to get to Jerusalem. I have many disciples to see." Their pace quickens.

The city is so close that they hear the faint cries of the merchants and marketers hawking their wares. The men walk for about fifteen minutes in silence.

`Isa says, "Jesus, I think this is where I must leave you. I'm not going into the city. I have a different mission."

"What's that? Where are you going?" Jesus asks.

"I'm being raised up to our Lord himself."[14]

"'Taken back,'" Jesus says. "You mentioned earlier you were to be 'taken back' to the Lord. Your ministry is finished until you come again sometime in the future."

`Isa, nodding his head, says, "That's right."

Jesus says, "Thank you for an afternoon well spent. It was good to hear what you had to say. It is important to understand how different we are, after all. So I hope you'll excuse me while I hurry to the great city. My work continues."

`Isa nods. "Yes, and my work ends—for now."

Jesus turns to the city and with a confident stride is soon very near the Gate Beautiful. One last time he turns around to see what has happened to `Isa. `Isa is gone. Not a trace remains of him. It's as if he never existed.

Jesus chuckles to himself, "Let's go give the disciples another visit. At least they'll know who I am."

Appendix A

Physical Descriptions of Jesus in Islamic Sources

- Resembles Urwah ibn Mas`ud (Sahih al-Muslim 321, 328, 7023).
- Ruddy complexion, curly hair, and broad chest (Sahih al-Bukhari 4:648).
- Red face, average height (and he had just come from the bathroom) (Sahih al-Bukhari 4:607, 647).
- Did not have a red complexion, but had brown and lanky hair, in contradistinction to *al-Dajjal* (the antichrist) who had a red complexion, curly hair, and was blind in the right eye (Sahih al-Bukhari 4:650).
- He was a curly-haired man of moderate height (Sahih al-Bukhari 4:608).
- He was of medium height, moderate complexion, and his hair was lanky with red and white colors (Sahih al-Bukhari 4:462).
- Sweating while circumambulating the *Ka'ba*, he is said to have lanky hair (Sahih al-Bukhari 4:649).

- Sweating while circumambulating the *Ka'ba*, he is a whitish-brown man, handsomest of all brown men, beautiful with long hair (*limma*: hair hanging to earlobes) that was combed (Sahih al-Bukhari 7:789).
- Sweating while circumambulating the *Ka`ba*, he is whitish-red, handsomest of that complexion, hair reaching his earlobes that was the best of such hair and was combed (Sahih al-Bukhari 9:128).

Why Provide Descriptions of Jesus?

The time span between the drying of the ink of the Bible (ca. AD 90) and that of the earliest hadith (ca. AD 780) is nearly 700 years. This one fact raises many questions that demand examination:

1. If the eyewitness accounts of the Gospels are closer to the real Jesus than Islamic sources, why are there no physical descriptions of him in the Gospels?

2. Why do we find much, much later Islamic documents providing physical descriptions of Jesus? What reasons are there for knowing what he looked like?

3. Perhaps the most important question: Which source are we going to accept as legitimate? Which of the documents gives us an accurate description of Jesus?

Why Are There No Physical Descriptions of Jesus in the New Testament?

The answer is fairly straightforward. There are relatively few physical descriptions of *any* person in the Scriptures. These appear only where the author believes such a description is necessary to drive the story or to serve the author's purpose. Characters in the biblical chronicle are more often illustrated in terms of their character, attitudes, thoughts, and behaviors than with physical imagery. The following is a partial list of individuals given any type of physical description. Though partial, it is an accurate index of how Scripture's authors dealt with character development in their stories. There is an emphasis on inner life and personal qualities rather than an accent on appearance:

- Adam and Eve: Naked living beings (Genesis 2:7, 25) who later wear fig leaves and then the skin of animals (3:7, 21).
- Cain: Tiller of the soil (Genesis 4:2) with a fallen countenance (4:5) who later becomes a wanderer (4:12ff).
- Abel: Keeper of flocks (Genesis 4:2).
- Seth: Born in the likeness of Adam (Genesis 5:3).
- Sarai/Sarah: Beautiful (Genesis 12:11; implied in 20:2).
- Abram/Abraham: Rich in livestock, in silver and gold (Genesis 13:2).
- Rebekah: Very beautiful (Genesis 24:16).
- Esau: Red and hairy (Genesis 25:25; Jacob is not described in any manner at his birth, though he is later described as "a quiet man," living in tents, v. 27).
- Leah: Weak eyes (Genesis 29:17).
- Rachel: Lovely in form and beautiful (Genesis 29:17).
- Moses: Beautiful as a baby (Exodus 2:2).
- Eglon, king of Moab: Very fat (Judges 3:17).
- Samson: Long hair (Judges 16:17; Samson is never described as muscle-bound, or in any other physical manner).
- Saul: Impressive and without equal, taller than anyone (1 Samuel 9:3).

- David: Ruddy, with a fine appearance and handsome features (1 Samuel 16:12).
- Goliath: Over nine feet tall (1 Samuel 17:4).

The list could go on, but I think you get the idea. The biblical authors crafted their stories around people whose physical description would, more often than not, get in the way, drag down the story, or offer unimportant detail. Go back and see how the authors develop the interpersonal relationships among Adam, Eve, and God; between Noah and his family; or between Saul and Samuel. These relationships are the nexus of each story. The stories do not need physical descriptions of the main characters.

Why Do We Find Descriptions of Jesus (and Muhammad) in Islamic Sources but Not in Christian Sources?

Might it be possible that as a community moves away from its prophet/messiah, the need becomes greater for personal characteristics to become clearer, to visualize the person, to keep the person's memory alive, and to help the followers maintain some allegiance?

There is some merit in this idea, but it does not fully answer the question. There are many descriptions of Muhammad in the hadith. The above theory may account for descriptions of Muhammad's physical attributes, but not of Jesus'. Jesus is 700 years in the past. There was no reason to try to understand what Jesus looked like—unless of course he was made to look like Muhammad. In fact, it is most likely that portrayals of all the biblical prophets were built on the character of Muhammad. Muhammad stands as a template for each previous prophet. As the final messenger, a prophet *magna cum laude*, he sums up all the previous voices of God. What we find in the Qur'an are many deliberate comparisons of biblical prophets with Muhammad. It is as if the life of Muhammad is read back into the lives of the biblical prophets. This is neither a dark secret nor an intentional deception on the part of the author(s) of the Qur'an. However, it is undeniably true that Muhammad stands as *the* pinnacle of prophets, *the* crowning achievement of their characters, *the* model of their methods and manners. Christians speak of Jesus as the fulfillment of the Law. For Muslims, Muhammad stands as the final installment and embodiment of all that is best of the prophets. So Jesus is described as an important prophetic predecessor of Muhammad in Islamic sources.

Which Documents Can We Trust for Authentic Information about Jesus?

This question is painfully simple: the biblical account is undisputedly closer to the Jesus of the first century than are descriptions of the `Isa of the seventh century.

The religion of Islam did not drop out of the sky fully formed, finely tuned and ready for Muhammad and the first Muslims. No religion does! The Arabian Peninsula was awash in animism, polytheism, and a nascent Arabic monotheism. Even Judaism and Christianity were known among the Arabs of the sixth century. Before this evolving Islam—an Islam that had an Islamic Jesus—claimed the allegiance of Arabs, there existed written descriptions of Jesus in apocryphal and pseudepigraphal literature.

There are two threads I want to weave into the fabric of the Islamic context: orthodox christology and popular Christianity. What was the church saying about Jesus during the centuries leading up to Islam, and what literature was written for "popular" consumption (although often foisting itself off as authentically penned by an apostle)?

Second-century christology mostly centered on the reality of Jesus. This was a debate fueled by the Gnostics, who posited that Jesus only *seemed* to be real. After all, they argued, how could one who was divine debase himself by becoming trapped in a physical body?

But what did the church believe? According to Irenaeus,

> The Church, though dispersed throughout the whole world, even to the ends of the earth, has received from the apostles and their disciples this faith: [She believes] in one God the Father Almighty, Maker of heaven, and earth, and the sea, and all things that are in them; and in one Christ Jesus, the

Son of God, who became incarnate for our salvation; and in the Holy Spirit, who proclaimed through the prophets the dispensations of God, and the advents, and the birth from a virgin, and the passion, and the resurrection from the dead, and the ascension into heaven in the flesh of the beloved Christ Jesus, our Lord.[1]

Jesus was the incarnated God, a physical manifestation of the Almighty. He was not a phantom.

On the other hand, popular Christianity was concerned more about the early days of Jesus, his relations to his mother, and the twelve years prior to his appearance at the temple. Such questions drove the production of the *Infancy Gospel of Thomas*, perhaps as early as mid–second century, and the *Infancy Gospel of James*, also known as the *Protoevangelium of James*, a title that implies this text was the "prequel" to the canonical Gospels. Its earliest manuscript is from the tenth century. These "infancy gospels" provided fairy tale–like stories about the holy family that tickled the fancy of many believers.

As christological questions developed in the third and fourth centuries, the literature produced by Christians reflected these concerns. There is the *Gospel of St. Matthew*, a Latin work translated by St. Jerome, containing even more wondrous miracles about Jesus than would be thought possible in order to explain his early years, family relationships, and his own nature. The *Arabic Gospel of the Infancy* was popular among Nestorian Christians in the fourth and fifth centuries, but it seems impossible to date.

As the birth of Islam drew close in early eighth century, christological developments focused on the unity of Christ's human and divine natures. The Council of Ephesus decided in favor of Cyril over against Nestorius in 431. Nestorian Christians were then confirmed as heretics by the Council of Chalcedon in 451. Why? The extreme Nestorian view, from the orthodox perspective, held to a Jesus who was two persons, human and divine, with no unity. The significance of this for us is that Nestorian Christianity did not go away. It spread throughout the East, probably including Arabia. It is quite likely that much of the Arab understanding of the Christian Jesus was from a form of Nestorian Christianity.

By the time Muhammad arrived in the seventh century, Christians had debated christology for nearly six hundred years! There were many streams of Christian thought about Jesus, and one of them seems to have found its way into the Qur'an. Muhammad's understanding of Jesus reflected a sixth- and seventh-century understanding of Jesus rather than the first-century Jesus. That is, the `Isa of the Qur'an is not the Jesus of the Bible, but one whose character and attributes mirror a Jesus of a different time, place, and context.

If this is the case, the documents in which one may find relevant and authentic information about Jesus cannot be from the seventh and eighth centuries. The relevant manuscripts must be first-century documents—as is the case with the New Testament record. The Qur'an is much later and therefore displays an understanding of a Jesus philosophically located within the sixth and seventh centuries. The only conclusion possible is that the documents of the New Testament portray a first-century Jesus far more accurately than any Islamic document, including the Qur'an.

A Summary of the Qur'anic Jesus

The Qur'an has 6,226 verses. Only 93 mention `Isa. This means that `Isa is *not* a concern of the Qur'an about 98.5% of the time. True enough, the Qur'an presents him as an honorable prophet, yet he is merely another prophet in the long line of people who preceded the final prophet of Islam, Muhammad. It is in this light, vis-à-vis Muhammad, that the real significance of Jesus must be seen.

In my story, `Isa is constantly hitting on one of the major themes of the Qur'an: the oneness of Allah. There is no one like Allah. He has no partners. He shares himself with no one and nothing. To make Allah a partner or sharer with anyone is to commit the unforgivable sin, *shirk*. As one of many prophets sent by Allah to his people, `Isa espouses the same creed. All things are his, all people are his. Allah is the owner of everything. Those who deny the oneness of Allah are *kafr*, which besides meaning an unbeliever also connotes ungratefulness. The man or woman who refuses to make the oneness of Allah his or her guide for life expresses a lack of appreciation and indebtedness for who Allah is. The ungrateful person, the *kafr*, feels no obligation to worship or to submit himself or herself to Allah. This is serious business.

This is the message of `Isa. He is, as John the Baptist was to Jesus the Messiah, a forerunner of the prophet to come, Ahmad. `Isa's message, lifestyle, and speech are adumbrations of Ahmad/Muhammad.

So, who is `Isa in the Qur'an, really?

- He brought a covenant with Allah (33:7). This covenant does not appear to be similar in any way to the covenant Yahweh established with Israel in the Hebrew Scriptures or the new covenant established through the death, burial, and resurrection of the Messiah.
- He is a sign of the coming hour (21:90; 23:50; 43:57–61).
- He cursed the Jews (5:78). Both Jesus and David curse the Jews for their disobedience and excess. In the verse immediately following, the Jews are further condemned for rejecting Muhammad as the prophet of Islam (5:81). Also in the immediate context is the statement that nearest to the Muslims are the Christians because they are men devoted to learning and who shun this world (5:82).
- He had disciples (3:52–54; 5:111–13; 57:27; 61:14). His disciples are never named and are simply presented in a parallel version to the helpers, the people of Medina who pledged their support to Muhammad. His disciples had to admit to having faith in Jesus, but additionally submit themselves to Allah in Islam.
- He predicted the coming of Ahmad (61:6). This may be the real function of `Isa in the Qur'an. Many Christians, it was thought, would pledge their allegiance to Muhammad if it could be shown that their prophet, Jesus, had prophesied the coming of another prophet.
- He was the son of Mary (4:75, et al.).
- He was called "Messiah" (4:75, et al.).

- He was one of the righteous prophets (6:85).
- He was only human and a messenger (4:171; 5:75; 43:59).
- He was a word from Allah (4:171). He was not the Word of Allah as Christians say he is the Word of God. He was a created person in Islam, like everyone else.
- He was a Spirit proceeding from Allah (4:171). This is not some hidden Trinitarian concept in the Qur'an. He was special, but still a created being.
- He served and worshiped Allah (4:172; 19:30; 43:63).
- He was a messenger for Israel only (3:49–51: 43:59). He was their example of how a person serves and worships Allah.
- He was raised to Allah rather than dying on the cross (3:55; 4:159). Some commentators have equated this to an Islamic version of the ascension.
- He was a Muslim (42:13). The religion Allah gave to Noah, Abraham, Moses, Jesus, and then Muhammad was Islam.
- He was given revelation (2:87, 136, 253; 3:48, 84; 4:163; 5:46; 19:30). He was given one book, the *Injil*. He is also included in a list of prophets who received revelation (not necessarily books).
- He is not Allah (5:17, 72; 9:30–31). It is blasphemy to associate Jesus with Allah (*shirk*). He especially is *not* the son of Allah. Jesus openly commanded the Jews to worship only Allah.
- He performed miracles (3:49; 5:110, 113–15). He created a bird from clay, provided food from heaven, gave sight to the blind, and healed lepers.
- He spoke from the cradle (3:46; 5:110; 19:30–33).
- He will testify before Allah (5:116–18). The time seems to be the Day of Judgment when Allah will ask Jesus if he ever told his followers to worship him and his mother. Jesus will adamantly deny it and affirm the oneness of Allah.
- He told the Jews to fear Allah and to obey him, Jesus (43:63).

Christians naturally gravitate to any mention of Jesus in the Qur'an. There are many similarities and likenesses between `Isa and Jesus. A list of those similarities might be as follows:

- He was born of a virgin.
- He was the son of Mary.
- He performed miracles.
- He was called "Messiah."
- He was given revelation.
- He said to fear God and to obey him, Jesus.
- He served and worshiped God.
- He had disciples.
- He was raised to Allah.

These similarities are significant, but are they enough for Christians—or Muslims for that matter—to say that there is only one Jesus? Similarities are not enough to dispel the differences that exist:

- `Isa had no connection to the temple, Torah, or the kingdom of heaven.
- `Isa was never more than a foreshadowing of Muhammad.
- `Isa's message did not include reconciliation, forgiveness, restoration, covenant, or any other major biblical theme.
- `Isa never spoke of Allah as his Father, let alone Yahweh.
- `Isa was never called Immanuel, Son of God, Lamb of God, Son of Man, and other biblical titles for Messiah.
- If the above are not sufficient, there is still one more critical difference: `Isa neither died on the cross nor rose from the dead.

Muslims will continue to insist they love Jesus. I think it's futile to respond, "No you don't!" as if Christians were the only people to know about Jesus. Why not respond, "I'm glad you do. Tell me why." You might find yourself at the beginning of a God-appointed friendship in which you will have many opportunities to tell the story of Jesus—the real Jesus.

Endnotes

Introduction

1. The traditions of Islam, or *hadith*, are stories of Muhammad and his closest companions. Muhammad is the supreme example of how to live a life that is submitted to Allah, and these stories help Muslims know what is allowed and what is prohibited. Further, these traditions provide some context for a proper interpretation of the Qur'an.

2. The biography of Muhammad, *Sirat Rasul Allah*, is an authoritative source for the life of Muhammad. Written by Ibn Ishaq, it was redacted two hundred years after the death of Muhammad. Nevertheless, Alfred Guillaume, the translator of the *Sirat*, believes the biography "is recorded with honesty and truthfulness and, too, an impartiality which is rare in such writings." *The Life of Muhammad: A Translation of Ishaq's Sirat Rasul Allah* (Karachi: Oxford, 1955), xxiv.

3. *Anthills of the Savannah* (London: Heinemann, 1987).

Prologue

1. See Appendix A.

2. With apologies to Madeleine L'Engle.

Chapter 1: Introductions

1. Each chapter in the Qur'an is called a *surah*. The surah number is followed by the verse number. All qur'anic citations are from `Abdullah Yusuf `Ali, *The Meaning of the Holy Qur'an* (Beltsville, Md.: Amana Publications, 1989) unless otherwise stated.

2. All citations from Bukhari are from ISL Software Corporation's `Alim 6.0 software. In turn, these are the translations from Muhammad Muhsin Khan, *The Translation of the Meanings of Sahih Al-Bukhari*, 9 volumes (Medina: Dar Ahya us-Sunnah al Nabawiya, 1971). The first number is the volume, followed by the number of the tradition. Sahih al-Bukhari is one of the six canonical *hadith* collections of Sunni Islam. These prophetic traditions, or hadith, were collected by the Muslim scholar Muhammad ibn Ismail al-Bukhari (AD 810–870) about 200 years after Muhammad died, and compiled during his lifetime. Most Muslims view this as their most trusted collection of hadith, and it is considered the most authentic book after the Qur'an. *Sahih* translates as *authentic* or *correct*.

3. Unless otherwise stated, all biblical citations are from the *Holy Bible, New International Version® NIV®*. Copyright © 1973, 1978, 1984 by Biblica, Inc.™. Used by permission of Biblica, Inc.™. All rights reserved worldwide.

4. That `Isa ever grinned, smiled, laughed, cried, or showed any explicit emotion is completely absent from the Qur'an and most authoritative hadith (from now on, *traditions*). He is pictured as a serious, somber, pious, ascetic-like figure that does not laugh or smile. In a tradition collected by al-Tawhidi (d. after AD 1010): "Jesus came upon his disciples and found them laughing. He said, 'He who fears [God] does not laugh.' They said, 'Spirit of God, we were only jesting.' Jesus replied, 'A person of sound mind does not jest.'" In Tarif Khalidi, *The Muslim Jesus: Sayings and Stories in Islamic Literature* (Cambridge: Harvard University Press, 2001), 144. I am taking liberty, however, to include such minimal emotion on his part.

5. Neither the Qur'an nor the traditions mention anything about Nazareth. The Qur'an only has one episode from Jesus' young life, and the location is unspecified.

6. Arabic speakers understand the derivation of `Isa to be from *Esau*. *Jesus* transliterated correctly would be *Yaso'a* or *Yushua*, not `Isa.

7. Mark 6:3.

8. The phrase "son of Mary" would not become common until Christianity spread into Syria. Among Syrian Christians, it was a title of honor. This could certainly account for the importance of the phrase among Arab Muslims 600 years after the Jesus of history.

9. Qur'an 4:171 (from now on the Qur'an will be signified by the letter Q). The first number is the *surah* or chapter, and the second is the *aya* or verse. All references to

the Qur'an are from A. Yusuf 'Ali, *The Meaning of the Holy Qur'an* (Beltsville, Md.: Amana Publications, 1989) unless otherwise noted.

10. Q4:172.

11. Q5:17.

12. Q19:31.

13. See *Sahih al-Bukhari* 2.440 (from now on *Sahih al-Bukhari* will be signified by the letter B, followed by the book number and hadith number).

14. Q3:67, 73, 85, 102; 5:3; 42:13, 21; 48:28; 61:9.

15. See Q1:1–7. This is the first chapter of the Qur'an. It is entitled al-Fatihah and its seven verses are a prayer for God's guidance, and stress his lordship and mercy. This chapter plays an essential role in daily prayers.

16. The Arabic *masih* comes from the root *masah*, "to touch."

17. There are no qur'anic or hadith references for 'Isa's going on the *hajj*. The commentators later attempted to attach this meaning to the title al-Masih, surmising that he must have performed the *hajj*.

18. Q3:45.

19. *Son of Man* is not found in the Qur'an or traditions. From this point forward, 'Isa's statements such as this one indicate the lack of qur'anic or traditional reference to the topic.

20. Ezekiel 2:1, 6, 8, et al.; Daniel 8:17. 1 Enoch and 4 Ezra, apocryphal intertestamental books, make many references to *son of man*. In the New Testament, *Son of Man* is found 82 times. D. E. Aune, "Son of Man," in *The International Standard Bible Encyclopedia*, ed. Geoffrey W. Bromiley (Grand Rapids: Eerdmans, 1988), 4:574–81.

21. Suggested by V. Taylor in Geoffrey Parrinder, *Jesus in the Qur'an* (New York: Oxford University Press, 1977), 32.

22. Q19:30.

23. Ibid.

24. Q19:19.

25. Q4:171.

26. Ibid.

27. Q3:43.

28. Q19:21.

29. Q4:157.

30. Q43:57 (The Arabic *mathal* can be translated as "parable").

31. Q3:43.

32. Q3:45, Pickthall's version. 'Ali translates *wajih* as "held in honor."

33. Q61:6.

34. Mark 8:31ff; Luke 22:37; Matthew 8:17.

35. Isaiah 42:1; 52:13–53:12.

36. John 12:32.

37. There is no qur'anic or hadith record of 'Isa's being in Emmaus.

38. Q3:46.

39. Mark 6:4, 15; 8:2; Luke 13:33; John 6:14.

40. Matthew 26:25; Mark 9:5; John 1:38.

41. Luke 8:24.

42. Matthew 8:19; Mark 5:35; Luke 3:12; John 11:28.

43. Matthew 16:13–16.

44. There are many Muslims who believe it was Paul who founded the Christianity we know today, a religion very different from the religion of Jesus (i.e., Islam). Today this charge to dismiss Jesus as divine is led, ironically, by biblical scholars and historians rather than by Muslims, viz., Marvin Meyers, Walt Eisenmann, and Bart Ehrman.

45. *Servant of the Lord* is *'Abdullah* in Arabic.

46. Isaiah 42:1.

47. Matthew 17:12; Mark 8:31; Luke 9:22.

48. Matthew 8:17.

49. Matthew 20:28.

50. John 1:29.

51. Luke 1:17.

52. Q19:7.

53. See Q19:12–15.

54. Acts 3:13, 26; 4:27, 30.

55. Q6:164; 16:25; 35:18; 53:38.

56. Q10:48; 13:8; 22:35; 23:46 (in some cases, *messenger* is translated as *apostle*).

57. Q38:1–5; 15:57ff; 61:6. Ahmad is Muhammad. Both come from the same root, *hmd*. See also B4:556. It seems extraordinary that 'Isa would know the name of the next prophet. This is certainly not the pattern of the biblical prophets.

58. Q57:27.

59. Q6:83–90. This is not a biblically accurate chronology of the prophets, but it is the order listed in the Q6:91–92.

60. There is no mention in the Qur'an or traditions that 'Isa ever knew of the Qur'an. But for the purposes of the story, I am giving him that knowledge. He will never quote directly from it, but will make qur'anically relevant and sympathetic statements.

61. Q34:28.

62. Malachi 3:1; Matthew 11:14; Mark 9:13; Luke 1:17.

63. Matthew 10:7.

Chapter 2: For Unto Us a Child Is Born

1. There is no mention of `Isa's father in the Qur'an. This story is from Abu al-Hajjaj al-Balawi, as in Khalidi, *The Muslim Jesus*, 196–97. al-Balawi was a scholar of the early thirteenth century. The mention of the screen is an Islamic understanding of the proper code of conduct between men and women. For instance, the wives of Muhammad were required to be screened from men who were not from their immediate families (Q33:53 and B5:617). Even Mary screened herself (Q19:17).
2. A loose redaction of Q3:31–51.
3. Q19:27–30.
4. Q26:63, et al.
5. Q27:18–19.
6. B4:645. In each of the three situations it appears the author of the account has the child speaking in order to come to the aid of someone falsely accused of an immoral act.
7. Q3:59.
8. Q19:23–25.
9. Q19:27–34.
10. 1 Chronicles 24:10; Luke 1:5.
11. Luke 1:26.
12. Q5:75.
13. Here I am making reference to the *Infancy Gospel of James*. The book is of unknown authorship and its earliest manuscript, now in the Bodmer Library, Oxford, is dated to the third century. The beginning chapters contain stories about Mary's unusual birth and early days. In the final chapters of the book, Jesus is born, is hidden from Herod, and so forth. The book is an embellishment of the stories found in Matthew and Luke.
14. Q22:17.
15. Q85:21–22.
16. Q3:49.
17. Q7:157.
18. Q3:50.
19. Q5:110.
20. Q43:57–59.
21. Q61:14.
22. Q61:6.
23. Genesis 3:1–24.

24. Genesis 3:15.

25. Q18:38; 22:26.

26. Luke 4:18–19.

27. Isaiah 61:1–3.

28. Q5:116.

29. Proverbs 17:17.

Chapter 3: One More to Come

1. Q61:6.

2. Q5:14.

3. Q10:47; 4:163.

4. Deuteronomy 18:15–18.

5. I am aware that the prophecies of the coming Messiah include titles such as Immanuel (Isaiah 7:10); Wonderful Counselor, Mighty God, Everlasting Father, and Prince of Peace (Isaiah 9:6); the Lord and his Anointed One (Psalm 2:2); and the Son of Man (Daniel 7:13), but none of these are names as such.

6. Deuteronomy 34:10.

7. Q20:9–36; 28:29–35.

8. Exodus 3:15.

9. There are no early sources for this Islamic polemic. Neither the Qur'an, the *sirat* (biography) of Muhammad, nor the traditions equate the Comforter/*paraclete* with Muhammad. Nevertheless, I have put these words into the mouth of 'Isa because they represent a consistent (though hardly persuasive) argument presented by Muslims today.

10. The Arabic radical means "praise." John Penrice, *A Dictionary and Glossary of the Qur'an* (Des Plaines, IL.: Library of Islam, 1988), 38.

11. Here the Muslim polemic is as follows: Originally, the word *periklutos* (praised) was changed by Christians to *paraklētos* (comforter, advocate, intercessor) because they realized it spoke of the coming of Muhammad, the prophet of Islam.

12. Song of Songs 5:16. The simplified transliteration of the first two phrases is *khikô mam'taqim wekullô makhămadim*. This verse is the final word in which Muslims see the name Muhammad in the Bible. This is a very common argument presented by Muslims.

13. Song of Songs: "The expression 'Song of Songs . . . being a superlative." F. B. Knutson, "Canticles," in *The International Standard Bible Encyclopedia*, ed. Geoffrey W. Bromiley (Grand Rapids: Eerdmans, 1979), 1:606.

14. *Yodh-mem* ('-îm') are the final two letters to the noun *shirim*. These two letters are often posited by Muslims as a sign of respect. Thus *elohim* is "God" in a respectful form. This is a poorly planned plot on the part of polemicists.

15. *Jinn* are good and evil spirits (Q72).

16. *al-Rum* refers to the Romans or Byzantines (Q30).

17. *Rabb* is "lord" or "master" (Q1:4).

18. *Shātan* is found in 1 Samuel 25:22, 34; 1 Kings 14:10.

19. See Hosea 9:6, 16; 1 Kings 20:6; Lamentations 1:10, 11; 2:4; Isaiah 64:10; 2 Chronicles 36:19; Ezekiel 24:16, 21, 25, where the radical is a noun.

20. Q7:190.

21. Q57:4.

22. Q7:143.

23. The following story is found in B4:429, 640; 5:227; 9:608.

24. Q19:56ff. Idris is usually identified by Muslim scholars as Enoch.

25. al-Tirmidhi, hadith 247. The Mosque at Aqsa is the Jerusalem mosque. "My mosque" is the prophet's mosque in Medina. The Sacred Mosque is the Ka'ba in Mecca.

26. Jerusalem was not conquered by the Muslims until AD 638, six years after Muhammad's death. al-Aqsa was first built in AD 691–92. A. Yusuf 'Ali's commentary is helpful (to see the historical disconnect) for identifying the place Muhammad visited: "*The Farthest Mosque* must refer to the site of the temple of Solomon in Jerusalem on the hill of Moriah, at or near which stands the dome of the Rock. This and the mosque known as the Farthest Mosque (*Masjid al Aqsa*) were completed by the Amir 'Abd al Malik in A.H. 68." *The Meaning of the Holy Qur'an*, p. 673, n. 2168.

27. It was Abu Bakr who defended the truthfulness of Muhammad's Night Journey. Some left Islam at that time because they could not believe Muhammad had made such a journey, but Abu Bakr consistently stated he believed the story and the veracity of Muhammad. See A. Guillaume, *The Life of Muhammad: A Translation of Ibn Ishaq's Sirat Rasul Allah* (Karachi: Oxford University Press, 1955), 181–83.

Chapter 4: Wine, Women, and Song

1. al-Ghazali, in Tarif Khalidi, *The Muslim Jesus* (Cambridge: Harvard University Press, 2001), 167. He was an eleventh-century Muslim scholar, philosopher, and mystic.

2. Abu Uthman al-Jahiz, in *The Muslim Jesus*, 96.

3. Matthew 9:13.

4. *Hawa* is Arabic for Eve.

5. I am inserting the words of Muhammad into the mouth of Jesus. The prophet of Islam said, "But for Eve, wives would never betray their husbands" (B4:547). This is

something `Isa of the Qur'an would probably have believed because it was to come from the mouth of the final prophet.

6. Ahmad ibn Hanbal, in *The Muslim Jesus*, 86.

7. Paraphrase from Abu al-Hasan al Mawardi, in *The Muslim Jesus*, 161.

8. Kamal al-Din al-Damiri, in *The Muslim Jesus*, 206–9.

9. Abdallah ibn Qutayba, in *The Muslim Jesus*, 107.

10. "I was a witness over them whilst I dwelt amongst them" (Q5:117).

11. Ahmad ibn Hanbal, in *The Muslim Jesus*, 72.

12. Hadith Qudsi. This is one of forty traditions allegedly from Allah himself—stories, parables, proverbs, adages, etc. directly from the mouth of Allah, but not part of the Qur'an.

13. Mark 1:15.

14. Ahmad ibn Hanbal, in *The Muslim Jesus*, 78.

15. Ikhwan al-Safa', in *The Muslim Jesus*, 143–44. This is a fairly late saying attributed to Jesus in the tenth century. Ikhwan al-Safa' translates it as "brethren of purity/sincerity." See Nader el-Bizri, *Epistles of the Brethren of Purity: The Ikhwan as-Safa' and Their Rasa'il* (New York: Oxford University Press, 2009).

16. Ahmad ibn Hanbal, in *The Muslim Jesus*, 76. On this citation, Khalidi says, "Among modern educated Muslims, this is perhaps Jesus' best known saying. . . . This is the ascetic ideal at its most austere. The world as a dunghill is also an image employed by Muhammad."

17. Matthew 6:33.

18. Proverbs 9:10; 15:33.

19. Abdallah ibn al-Mubarak, in *The Muslim Jesus*, 55.

20. This story is found in Abu Bakr `Atiq Nayshaburi Surabadi, *Stories from the Holy Qur'an,* as cited in Jay R. Crook, *Jesus (The Bible: An Islamic Perspective)* (ABC International Group, 2005).

Chapter 5: Jots and Tittles

1. Matthew 21:18ff.

2. Q3:3.

3. Q5:48.

4. Q5:46.

5. Psalm 119:89.

6. Q15:9.

7. Q85:21–22.

8. Q5:48.

9. Q85:21–22.

10. Q5:41.

11. Jeremiah 7:4–8.

12. The irony of Jesus' answer is that I have put into his mouth the comment by A. Yusuf `Ali on the passage in question from his translation of the Qur'an (n. 746).

13. Q5:44.

14. Psalm 119:11.

15. This is not an insignificant argument. Muslims claim as evidence for the preservation of the Qur'an the fact that countless people have memorized the Qur'an, thus ensuring its integrity from the days of Muhammad to the present. Both the Jews and the early Christians had similar traditions of memorization.

16. Q35:32; 80:11–16.

17. Q5:22 (Torah); 26:196 (Psalms announce the coming of Qur'an); Q3:84 (Gospel).

18. Luke 1:1–4.

19. Mark 1:15.

20. Luke 4:18–19.

21. Matthew 5:17.

22. Genesis 15:6; Habakkuk 2:4; Acts 3:16.

23. Ezekiel 11:19; 36:26.

Chapter 6: Boys with Beetles

1. Q3:55. See also Q4:157 (the fabricated story of Jesus' crucifixion) and 5:116 (God corrects the impossible story that Jesus taught that he and his mother ought to be worshiped).

2. This story is found in the *Infancy Gospel of Thomas*, the *Arabic Infancy Gospel*, and the *Infancy Gospel of Pseudo-Matthew*.

3. Luke 3:21–22.

4. Luke 4:1–13.

5. Luke 4:16–30.

6. Translation and arrangement from Robert C. Tannehill, *The Narrative Unity of Luke-Acts* (Philadelphia: Fortress, 1986), 1:62.

7. *People of the Book* can refer to either Christians (Q3:65) or Jews (Q2:101).

8. B1:532.

Chapter 7: Did He or Didn't He Die?

1. This refers to revelation given to Muhammad during his early ministry in Mecca. Later he immigrated to Medina, where he received more revelation. The final era of his ministry was spent once again in Mecca.

2. Q19:15.

3. Q19:66–72; 23:35–38; 80:19–22.

4. Q4:155.

5. Q4:156.

6. Q2:154; see Parrinder, *Jesus in the Qur'an*, 113.

7. Q3:55.

8. Q5:17.

9. There are no qur'anic or traditional references to `Isa's being uneasy around dogs. It is an extrapolation from the life of Muhammad, who warned of having dogs as pets because they actually cause a person to lose spiritual rewards. Dogs as working animals were not a problem (B3:515; 7:389; 7:843). Also, a dog crossing between a person performing *salat* and the *qibla* nullifies the prayer (B1:490).

10. Q60:7.

11. For the following portion I owe a debt of gratitude to John Gilchrist.

12. Exodus 19:10.

13. Jeremiah 31:31–34.

14. Ezekiel 36:26–27.

15. Zechariah 3:8–9.

16. Matthew 9:1–8.

17. Q27:31; 61:9; B5:245, 250; Sahih al-Muslim 6945 (henceforth abbreviated as M).

18. These are two of the ninety-nine names of God. J. W. Sweetman writes that *al-Khaliim* (the Clement) "is often used in the Qur'an in a context expressing the forgiving acts of God." *Islam and Christian Theology*, vol. 2, part 1 (London: Lutterworth, 1947), 49. *al-Sabuur*, not found in the Qur'an, means "the Forbearing One, the Patient."

19. Q2:225–26; 5:98; 24:22; 35:28–29; B6:414.

20. Q4:110.

21. Luke 15:11–32.

22. Q3:31.

23. Q9:5.

24. Q5:73–74. *Shirk* is the Islamic sin of associating partners with Allah. Since he alone is the deity of the universe, no other—including Jesus—can be considered equal to Allah.

25. Q5:39.

26. Q25:70.

27. Q4:110.

28. Q9:99; 4:17.

29. The irony of Jesus' statement is that the ninety-nine names of God include *al-Mudhhill,* the Giver of Dishonor, Humiliater, Degrader (he is the One who leads astray). Q4:90; 4:142; 17:99; 18:6.

30. Q2:91; 3:21, 181.

31. Q2:136—Say ye: "We believe in Allah and the revelation given to us and to Abraham, Isma`il, Isaac, Jacob, and the Tribes and that given to Moses and Jesus and that given to [all] Prophets from their Lord, we make no difference between one and another of them and we bow to Allah [in Islam]." See also Q2:285, 3:84 and 4:152.

Chapter 8: A Grievous Penalty

1. al-Dunya, *Kitab al-Samt wa Adab al-Lisan,* in Khalidi, *The Muslim Jesus,* 123.

2. Ibid., 122. These proverbs were said by `Isa to show his disciples that they must avoid slander.

3. Proverbs 10:18.

4. Q39:4.

5. Q19:92.

6. Q112:1–4.

7. Deuteronomy 6:4: "Hear, O Israel: the LORD our God, the LORD is one."

8. Implied from Q19:34–35.

9. The Arabic phrase *son of the road* means a traveler.

10. Matthew 1:18.

11. Matthew 1:20.

12. Luke 1:35.

13. Q5:116.

14. B1:3; 4:605; 6:748.

15. Q2:144–146 (The People of the Book know Muhammad's teaching is true, even if they don't become Muslims); 3:113 and 29:47 (some of them are believers, i.e., Muslims).

16. This is patripassianism. The Messiah is the Father. Therefore, the Father was born, suffered, and died under Pontius Pilate. Its main proponent was Noetus in the early third century.

17. Literally *the god bearer,* but as applied to Mary it is often (mis)translated as *the mother of God.* The term was meant to speak to the unity of the two natures of Christ, but has perhaps brought about more division than unification.

18. Q5:73.

19. Q4:120.

20. Q7:22.

21. Exodus 3:1ff. I have opted to have Jesus discuss this theophany because the Qur'an has its own version. The next biblical theophany in which the Creator appears bodily is with Abraham (Genesis 18:1ff), but the Qur'an does not have its equivalent.

22. Q20:9ff.

23. Q27:8, 9. That Moses is told there are men in the fire is undoubtedly due to the author's confusion of two biblical events, the three Hebrew princes thrown into Nebuchadnezzar's fire (Daniel 3) and the burning bush.

24. Q28:30.

25. Genesis 3:14–15.

26. Q7:17; 35:6.

27. Isaiah 42:6.

28. Isaiah 49:6.

29. Isaiah 60:3.

30. Galatians 4:3–5.

31. John 4:23–24.

32. Matthew 5:17; Luke 24:44.

33. Isaiah 53:1–3; Matthew 16:21; 20:8; Mark 10:31–33, 45.

34. *Affectionate* is translated as *al-Wadud*; see Q85:14.

35. Q5:115–16.

36. The Qur'an confirms the previous revelations by preserving the truth of those revelations. Where the earlier texts agree with the Qur'an, the Qur'an is said to confirm them, but where they disagree, this to the Muslim is evidence of human tampering and corruption.

Chapter 9: The Last Hour

1. Q38:21–26.

2. Sahih al-Muslim 7015. This is one of the six major collections of traditions, or *hadith*, in Sunni Islam—oral traditions relating to the words and deeds of Muhammad. It is the second-most authentic hadith collection according to Sunni Muslims, the most authentic book of hadith after Sahih al-Bukhari. It was collected by Muslim ibn al-Hajjaj, also known as Imam Muslim. From now on it will be abbreviated by the letter M.

3. M6931.

4. M7015, 1370.

5. Q18:1.

6. B3:106.

7. M7015.

8. M6924.

9. M7015.
10. Cf. B4:556.
11. Cf. B6:236.
12. B3:425. *Jizya* is a tax levied only on the People of the Book. As part of the prosperity that 'Isa brings, the tax will no longer be necessary—especially since all Christians and Jews will then become Muslims.
11. Q5:3; 9:33; 27:31.
12. Q4:158.

Appendix B: Why Provide Descriptions of Jesus?
1. Irenaeus, *Against Heresies* I.10.1.

ALSO AVAILABLE

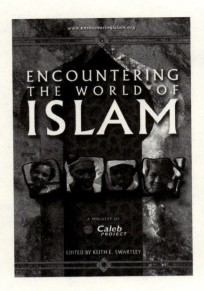

Encountering the World of Islam guides you on a journey into the lives of Muslims around the world and in your neighborhood. Through this comprehensive collection, you will learn about Muhammad and the history of Islam, gain insight into today's conflicts, and dispel western fears and myths. You will also discover the frustrations and desires of Muslims and learn how to pray for and befriend them. This book provides a positive, balanced, and biblical perspective on God's heart for Muslims and equips you to reach out to them in Christ's love.

Encountering the World of Islam features articles from eighty authors who have lived throughout the Muslim world, from West Africa to Southeast Asia. Experienced missionaries, scholars of Islam, and other well known authors, including several Muslims, contribute to this extensive ministry resource.

Features:
- Highlights in each lesson provide insight into Muslim culture, the Qur'an, and Muslim women.
- Discussion questions and other assignments will deepen your understanding as you reach out to Muslims with the love of Christ.
- Charts, maps, and illustrations illuminate the text and provide additional context.
- An extensive, easy-to-use glossary clarifies Muslim terminology.

Paperback, 618 pages, 6 x 9
ISBN: 978-1-93280-524-6
Retail: $39.99

Available for purchase at book retailers everywhere.

ALSO AVAILABLE

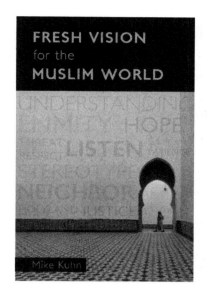

After living for more than two decades in the Middle East, pastor, author and college Arabic instructor Mike Kuhn wonders if there can be a fresh vision for the Muslim world—one not rooted in media lies or personal fears but in the values of Christ's kingdom. Is the only option to fight, to eradicate, to judge? Or can the mindset of confrontation give way to one of incarnation?

In *Fresh Vision for the Muslim World*, Mike Kuhn challenges readers to love the Muslims down the street and across the world with the love of Christ. Kuhn's vast experience and research show readers that Muslims today have the same hopes and spiritual needs as any of us. With practical suggestions, Kuhn helps readers leave the path of isolation, fear, and self-preservation and choose a less-traveled road: a path of self-awareness, empathy, and deep listening. Choosing the latter path is radical. It is difficult. And it is a step toward seeing Jesus Christ receive his rightful place of honor among a people longing to know him.

Paperback, 287 pages, 5.5 x 8.5
ISBN: 978-1-60657-019-7
Retail: $14.99

Available for purchase at book retailers everywhere.

ALSO AVAILABLE

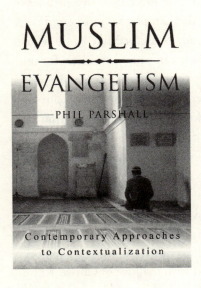

Too long the church has been pro-grammed to accept the inevitabilities of meager results in the efforts toward Muslim evangelization. The reasons for this failure in mission must now be probed and resolved as the world today is coming alive to the presence of the Muslim religious community. The author asks the missions world to forsake former pre-suppositions, and to become conscious of God speaking in a new and fresh manner—not in regard to his change-less Word—but in areas of extra-biblical methodology.

Dr. Parshall asks questions that explore the core of Christianity that is essential and what can be discarded in order to be an effective witness in the Muslim community.

This book has become the standard text for issues regarding contextualization of Christianity within the Islamic community.

Paperback, 320 pages, 5.5 x 8.5
ISBN: 978-1-88454-379-1
Retail: $12.99

Available for purchase at book retailers everywhere.

ALSO AVAILABLE

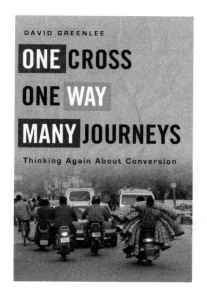

Conversion is at the core of Christian experience. Is it a process? Or can conversion be confined to a point in time? In our tolerance-driven, globalized world, should we even use the word at all? Social, political, and theological challenges push us to think again about this vital theme. Drawing on twenty-five years of mission experience, David Greenlee blends anthropological insights with evangelical theology to provide helpful missiological insights on conversion. He thoroughly illustrates the issue with cases and stories from South Asia where anti-conversion sentiment runs high, the Islamic world where the Law of Apostasy challenges any who would turn to Christ, and Europe where traditional religion and post-modern "tolerance" both confront any suggestion of conversion.

Paperback, 191 pages, 5.5 x 8.5
ISBN: 978-1-93280-577-2
Retail: $12.99

Available for purchase at book retailers everywhere.

ALSO AVAILABLE

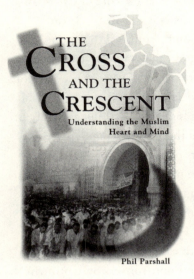

THE CROSS AND THE CRESCENT
Understanding the Muslim Heart and Mind

Phil Parshall

Phil Parshall addresses the question, How do we as Christians respond in faith and love to the Muslim people?

In this warm and personal book the author looks at what Muslims believe and how this affects—and often doesn't affect—their behavior. Phil Parshall compares and contrasts Muslim and Christian views on the nature of God, sacred scriptures, worship, sin, and holiness.

The Cross and the Crescent:

- Offers clear and concise insight into the world of Islam.
- Considers how Muslim's beliefs affect their behavior.
- Compares Muslim and Christian views on a number of issues.

Paperback, 320 pages, 5.5 x 8.5
ISBN: 978-1-88454-368-5
Retail: $12.99

Available for purchase at book retailers everywhere.